THE **DIARY**
OF A
domestic
diva

ALSO BY SHILPA SHETTY

The Great Indian Diet: Busting the Big Fat Myth
(with Luke Coutinho)

THE **DIARY** OF A *domestic diva*

90 mindful and heartful recipes from my kitchen

SHILPA SHETTY KUNDRA

Foreword by **SANJEEV KAPOOR**

EBURY
PRESS

An imprint of Penguin Random House

EBURY PRESS

USA | Canada | UK | Ireland | Australia
New Zealand | India | South Africa | China

Ebury Press is part of the Penguin Random House group of companies
whose addresses can be found at global.penguinrandomhouse.com

Published by Penguin Random House India Pvt. Ltd
7th Floor, Infinity Tower C, DLF Cyber City,
Gurgaon 122 002, Haryana, India

Penguin
Random House
India

First published in Ebury Press by Penguin Random House India 2018

ISBN 9780143440017

For sale in the Indian Subcontinent, United States of America,
United Kingdom and the Middle East only

Typeset in Adobe Caslon Pro by Manipal Digital Systems, Manipal
Printed at Thomson Press India Ltd, New Delhi

Dearest Daddy,
Wherever you are . . . Hope this makes you smile!

Contents

DESSERTS

YOGI BOWLS

PARTY MENUS

A DAY AT **VIVAMAYR**

Vegetarian recipe

You can watch this recipe on my YouTube channel

Foreword

What I like most about Shilpa's approach to food is that it's very honest. She belies the notion many of us have about stars: that they live by strict diets and don't eat as they please. Shilpa, as you will discover through this book, is a dedicated foodie and loves to eat. I have known her for a long time now and I can tell you that she certainly knows when to stop eating too, one of the key factors in maintaining a healthy body weight.

The Diary of a Domestic Diva is straight from her kitchen and offers a mix of healthy recipes, favourite recipes, famous recipes with a twist and guilt-free desserts. The idea behind the book is very heartening. It features recipes that do not take much of your time and leave you free to do other things. Through this book, she touches upon a beautiful point: Women need not be tied to the kitchen stove all day. Give a woman nutritious and fast-to-cook recipes and she will have the time to step out to do what she pleases. It's a cookbook with a message: Women ought to have some 'me' time. In my conversations with her, she has often mentioned the way, back in the day, her mother (a brilliant cook) would cook with the paucity of time as she was a working woman. I know it is all this that has led her to put together this book for the working woman. Being a family person, every aspect of her life draws from her experiences with people close to her. Her father's love for food and yet his fitness is another inspiration that has worked so well for her.

The recipes mentioned here have been tried out by her and I can vouch for their deliciousness. The fact that I drop everything when there's an invite to her lovely home for a meal is proof! The twists she adds to traditional recipes are delightful to say the least. *The Diary of a Domestic Diva* is about indulging your love for good food. And when such a message comes from one of the fittest people in town, you do sit up and take notice. Shilpa maintains that good food makes us happy and we shouldn't feel guilty about something that makes us happy, and over the years this is something I have come to believe too.

With this sure-to-be-a-bestseller cookbook, Shilpa also enters the space of celebrity cooks and it delights the chef in me to see the world get so interested in food. It is indeed one more brownie point for the food industry.

January 2018   Sanjeev Kapoor

Introduction

It's just bhindi. A vegetable that's probably as common as the potato in Indian homes. But at the mere mention of bhindi the first thing that pops in my mind is my sister. Shamita, for reasons she has sworn me to secrecy, abhors bhindi. No amount of masking it can get her to taste even a bite of the most delicious bhindi preparation. Her extreme reaction, and the fact that it is always discussed in my home, is why in every bhindi I see my beloved sister.

Food brings an onslaught of feelings, conjuring up some of our most powerful memories. In many cases, the taste or smell of a meal is capable of painting a picture more vibrant than any snapshot you may have on your phone. In other instances, it's the people sitting around you as you tuck in who make it a wonderful memory. Food that is linked with memorable events is more likely to trigger a few reminiscences than something we eat regularly, which is why we probably remember birthdays more clearly than the average Sunday brunch. Personally, it takes nothing more than a mutton dish to take me back to my childhood.

I grew up with parents who held full-time jobs. I remember my mother buying about 5 kilograms of chicken and 5 kilograms of mutton every weekend, cooking it all at once and freezing it. On alternate days, she would thaw a little bit after she came home from work and served it for dinner. I know many people who still do that—prepare the whole week's meals in advance. This book is for women like my mother who want to serve fresh, nutritious food to their families every day without spending too much time in the kitchen.

People probably think that just because I'm a celebrity, I diet a lot and don't eat what I want. But you know better than that from my previous book, *The Great Indian Diet*. I am a huge foodie and make and eat everything I like. The only difference is that I know when to stop. This book will show you how and what we—my husband, son and I—enjoy cooking at our home. I hope you like what we make.

Every dish you'll find in the pages that follow has been cooked by me. My family and I love each of these dishes and I enjoy making them, mainly because I can prepare them quickly, which leaves me free to attend to other tasks. As silly as it sounds, the most important thing for me while cooking is making sure my hair doesn't frizz. So the food I cook is usually very quick to make. And tasty, of course. I can't bear to cook recipes that involve a lot of preparation. They really put me off. I've gone through books where the pre-cooking instructions and ingredients are sometimes over one page long. Unless you're a professional cook, who has the energy to spend so much time getting so many ingredients ready? I certainly don't, and neither do most working women.

I don't claim that all the recipes here are original. Maybe you've already made some of them in your home. But each of them has a twist to it—something that makes it uniquely mine.

Before you begin reading this book, I want you to make a resolution: that you will enjoy every part of the meal—yes, that includes dessert too—without ever feeling guilty. The food we love and eat makes us so happy. Why would you feel guilty about feeling happy? My father loved, really loved, to eat good food. He was the kind of person who would attend the wedding of even a very distant relative of a relative (bless him!) because he wanted to sample the rich food served there. But it was also because he could never say no to an invitation. When he passed away recently, we wanted to celebrate him and his life. According to Mangalorean customs, the whole family comes home on the thirteenth day after the loved one has passed away for the Bojja ritual and eats vegetarian food. But my father was not fond of vegetarian food at all. For him, a meal was never complete unless it had a chicken or a mutton dish. Mutton was his most favourite meat and he relished every mutton dish that was ever served to him. He loved it so much that even if he was too busy to meet me, I could lure him home by saying I was cooking mutton! So for the evening of the thirteenth day, we prepared all of my father's favourite dishes and ended up with around twenty-one nonvegetarian dishes, including mutton cooked in four different ways. But despite his indulgences, he was a very fit man till the day he passed away. I believe it was because he took so much joy in eating and balanced it with his walks and yoga.

Every woman is domesticated in one way or the other because we are conditioned to make sure that we look after everyone around us. But in doing so we often neglect ourselves or feel apologetic for the things we do for ourselves. Being a professional, a wife and a mom is a tough job, and given the fast pace of our lives, we have to learn to compartmentalize. The glam quotient from our lives goes away when we become so domesticated. It's a beautiful coincidence that the Marathi word for lamp is 'diva'. Each one of us has a diva within us. I hope that through this book, I'm able to turn all of you into real-life divas and light the lamp inside you; I hope I can make your life simpler. Things like having an in-house menu can make figuring out what to prepare for lunch and dinner, pack for your husband and child and serve at parties easier. People may assume that I have it easy because I have plenty of help. On the contrary, being a homemaker comes first on my list and it's the finer details that make me a domestic diva. If these ideas can make life easier for you, I'll be so happy. And in that one hour that I'll be able to save in your day, I hope you go for a massage or get a pedicure or work out—do something for *your*self.

I hope this book makes your lives easier and with that also intend to bring focus to 'label reading'. Visiting the supermarket or vegetable vendor to buy your groceries every week may get cumbersome but your own and your family's health and what goes into your body must be of paramount importance. With readymade meals and pre-packaged quick fixes so easily available, I hope you don't take your family's lives for granted. Please read the label of the packet/box to know what has gone into it. Children should not be encouraged to eat sugary cereals and snacks on a regular basis; google it and you will know how harmful it can be. Reading the labels on packaged food products will also increase your knowledge and help you understand the difference between healthy and unhealthy food products. If you want to lead a healthy life, mindful eating is imperative.

With love, from my kitchen to yours.

Juices

SHILPA'S MANTRA

There is a school of thought that believes eating the whole fruit is better than consuming just its juices. I think that as long as you have juices at least 20 minutes before any meal and only up to 6 p.m., it can't do you harm. I also believe in the health benefits of raw vegetable juicing and have such juices regularly every mid-morning. Research says they aid overall system cleansing and are good for your hair and skin. I'm not a nutritionist, but I do know that randomly mixing anything to make a juice is not always the best because some foods are not compatible with each other. Your body finds it hard to digest certain juices. But if you add a bit of fat in the juice, it helps balance out the acidity raw juice might cause. That's why I've begun to put a teaspoon of olive oil, flaxseed oil or coconut oil in my juices. Now I don't feel bloated after having my daily juice. I used to suffer from a lot of acidity earlier. But now with a lot of trial and error, I've learned how to make my body more alkaline. The juices in the book not available in the market, along with my secret ingredient—oil—will do wonders for your body.

Mint and Lemon Juice ✿ ▶

This is a simple but effective recipe. This juice is the first thing we offer our guests and it's my speciality. I came up with this recipe because I hated the idea of serving aerated drinks to my guests. And since then, I never have. There are more juices that will follow a little later in the book. But since I welcome my guests with this mint and lemon juice, I welcome you to my book with it as well.

Serves: 2
Nutritional value: 36 kcal
(Carbs: 2 g, Protein: 1 g,
Fats: 3 g)

2 glasses water
1 tbsp ginger juice
Juice of 1½ lemon
Jaggery, to taste
¼ tsp rock salt
¼ tsp black pepper powder
1 cup ice cubes
Salt, to taste
2 tsp soaked
chia seeds
2–3 sprigs of mint leaves
A few lemon slices

1. In a mixer jar, add all the ingredients except the mint leaves and lemon slices, and mix them well.
2. Garnish with mint leaves and lemon slices.

Green Juice ✿

Cucumber, apple and pineapple are full of nutrients. When added to juices, cucumber is intensely alkalizing and offsets the acidic effects of sugar, aiding detoxification. Full of powerful antioxidants, apples are known to lower cholesterol and enhance digestion. Pineapples have immense health benefits, but are rather undervalued. Apart from mineral and vitamins, particularly vitamin C—one serving of pineapple has 130 per cent of our daily vitamin C requirement—they are rich in Bromelain, an enzyme that breaks down complex proteins and has great anti-inflammatory effects that help in reducing arthritis-related pain and swelling.

Serves: 2
Nutritional value:
161 kcal (Carbs: 29 g,
Protein: 0 g, Fats: 5 g)

1 cucumber
½ apple
½ cup pineapple chunks
5–6 tulsi or basil leaves
1 tsp flaxseed oil

1. Blend all the ingredients along with two pieces of ice and strain before drinking it.

ABCG Red Juice ✿

This is the mother of all juices, at least for me. It is great to detoxify, strengthen your eyes, liver, kidney, pancreas and immunity, maintain a healthy blood pressure and avoid constipation. Ginger improves digestion and helps cure acne, fight bad breath, promote hair growth and acts as an antidote for coughs and colds. So many pros and so yummy . . . why wouldn't you have it!

Serves: 1
Nutritional value:
130 kcal (Carbs: 28 g,
Protein: 0 g, Fats: 2 g)

½ red apple, chopped
½ beetroot, chopped
1 carrot, chopped
½ inch ginger, grated
½ tsp flaxseed or linseed oil or coconut oil

1. Blend all the ingredients and strain before drinking.

SHILPA'S TIP: If you find the ginger too pungent for your taste, you can reduce its quantity. The sweetness of the beets and apple will tone it down anyway.

Summer Juice 🌿

This juice is perfect in the summer to cool down the system and not feel sapped of energy.

Serves: 2
Nutritional Value:
63 kcal
(Carbs: 8 g, Proteins: 1 g,
Fats: 3 g)

¼ bottle gourd
½ apple, chopped
5 tulsi leaves
1 tsp chia seeds
½ tsp flaxseed oil

1. Blend all the ingredients and strain before drinking it.

SHILPA'S MANTRA

Potluck parties are always so much fun. They're the perfect setting for working people. You don't have to cook a lot—just one dish from everyone is enough.

Tea

SHILPA'S MANTRA
Colon cleanse 🌱

This juice cleanses your colon and flushes out built-up waste by rehydrating old stool and loosening it up so that it can be passed more easily. That way, it helps you to lose your water weight. A lot of people feel bloated and think they've put on weight. In such cases, this colon cleanse is perfect. You can carry it with you to work, or sip it on the way. It's convenient and effective.

1 tbsp maple syrup
Juice of ½ lemon
A pinch of cayenne pepper or black pepper powder
300 ml water

1. Mix everything in a jar and sip on this every day for 10 days.

Orange and Turmeric Tea

This is a concoction I have regularly. Even though it has turmeric, you can't taste it because of the oranges. Together, the oranges, with their high vitamin C content, and the turmeric, with its antibacterial and antibiotic properties, make this tea an excellent immunity booster and antidote to colds and coughs.

Serves: 2
Nutritional value: 26 kcal
(Carbs: 4 g, Protein: 0 g,
Fats: 0 g)

4 orange slices with rind
2 lemon slices
½ tsp turmeric powder
¼ cinnamon stick
500 ml hot water
1 tsp honey

1. Combine all the ingredients in a jar. Stir and mix for a minute and drink hot.

SHILPA'S MANTRA

Urinary tract infection is very common among Indian women, especially in the heat. One way to avoid that is to have barley. Boil 2–3 tbsp of pearl barley in 500 ml of water. Add some lemon juice and black pepper powder and keep sipping on it the whole day.

Saunf Tea 🌱

This tea is great for flatulence. I had it after my pregnancy. It helped me a lot with lactation and also brought down bloating.

Serves: 2
Nutritional value:
30 kcal (Carbs: 1 g,
Protein: 0 g, Fats: 0 g)

500 ml water
1 tbsp aniseed
½ tsp carom seeds

1. Boil all the ingredients. Strain and serve.

SHILPA'S SECRET: Add a smidgen of jaggery if you like your tea sweet.

Soups

Chicken Soup with Carrot and Celery

This soup is a whole meal in itself. I often make it for dinner. If you wish to, you can add a couple of tablespoons of cooked brown rice to it. I prefer chicken with bones than without because it's more nutritious and adds flavour.

Serves: 2
Nutritional value:
498 kcal (Carbs: 42 g,
Protein: 60 g, Fats: 10 g)

2 tsp vegetable oil
½ onion, chopped
1 bay leaf
300 g chicken, with bone
1 carrot, chopped
1 potato, cut into 4
(optional)
½ celery stick
2 sprigs of coriander
1 cube of chicken stock
(optional) (diluted in
3 tbsp water)
Water, to boil

1. In a cooker, heat the oil for a couple of minutes. Add the chopped onion and sauté it. Then add the bay leaf. Cook for about 10 minutes.

2. Add the chicken. Add the carrot, potato and celery and boil. Add a chicken stock cube if you like.

3. After about 10 minutes, take out the chicken and the bay leaf and blend the soup.

4. Shred the meat from the bones and add it back into the soup.

SHILPA'S SECRET: Vegetarians can replace the chicken stock cube with vegetable stock. They can also add a lot more greens like pak choi and broccoli. Adding grilled paneer will also make the soup taste wonderful.

Pumpkin Soup 🌱

Yellow pumpkin is my favourite vegetable. I have it when I'm happy and I have it when I'm feeling a bit low. It's a diuretic, so great for our health too. I love it in all forms and one of the best I've tasted is this pumpkin soup.

Serves: 4
Nutritional value:
350 kcal (Carbs: 20 g,
Protein: 0 g, Fats: 30 g)

2 tbsp vegetable oil or
coconut oil
1 cup chopped onion
1 cup diced celery
1 cup diced carrots
3 tbsp minced garlic
½ yellow pumpkin,
chopped
1 litre vegetable stock

1. Heat the oil in a cooker pot over medium heat. Add the onion, celery and carrot, stirring and cooking for about 15 minutes, until the vegetables soften. Stir in the garlic and cook for 1 minute.

2. Add the pumpkin and the vegetable stock and boil for another 10 minutes. Mash the pumpkin.

3. Add the seasonings and pass the soup through a sieve to take out the lumps.

1 tsp salt (check if your
vegetable stock has salt
in it)
½ tsp freshly ground black
pepper powder
½ tsp cayenne pepper
¼ cup fresh coriander,
finely chopped
2 tbsp grated coconut
(optional)

4. Garnish with grated coconut and serve.

SHILPA'S SECRET: You can add some warm milk or warm water if you find the soup thick. You can also make this a Pumpkin and Chicken Soup by adding 250 g steamed deboned steamed chicken in it.

Carrot Soup 🌿

When I was twelve, I was told by the doctor to wear glasses because my eyesight had become weak. Someone told my mother at that time that having carrots would improve my eyesight. Since that day, I've had at least one raw carrot with every meal. And I've never worn glasses again.

Serves: 4
Nutritional value:
268 kcal (Carbs: 40 g,
Protein: 0 g, Fats: 12 g)

1 big onion, chopped
½ inch ginger, grated
1 bay leaf
2 tsp coconut oil
4 carrots, chopped
1 tsp ginger–garlic paste
¼ tsp cinnamon powder
½ tsp cayenne pepper
2 litre vegetable
(or chicken) stock
¼ tsp olive oil
A few sprigs of coriander

1. Heat the coconut oil in a pot and sauté the onions and ginger with the bay leaf.

2. Add the carrots, ginger–garlic paste, cinnamon powder, cayenne pepper and vegetable stock. Cook for 30 minutes and puree it in a blender.

3. Add the olive oil and top with the coriander. Serve hot.

SHILPA'S MANTRA
Juices to combat ailments

Stress: Banana, strawberry, pear
Indigestion: Pineapple, carrot, lemon, mint
Depression: Carrot, apple, spinach, beet
Arthritis: Carrot, celery, pineapple, lemon
Ulcer: Cabbage, carrot, celery, 5 tulsi leaves
Fatigue: Carrot, beet, green apple, lemon, spinach, ½ tsp coconut oil
Nervousness: Carrot, celery, pomegranate
Hangover: Apple, carrot, beet, lemon
Asthma: Carrot, spinach, apple, garlic, lemon
Kidney detox: Carrot, watermelon, cucumber, cilantro
Headache: Apple, cucumber, kale, ginger, celery
Cold: Carrot, pineapple, ginger, garlic, ½ lemon
Constipation: Carrot, apple, fresh cabbage, beet, flaxseeds (or ½ tsp flaxseed oil)
Healthy eyes: Carrot, celery
Kidney stone: Barley water, apple, watermelon, lemon
UTI: Barley water, lime
Arthritis: Carrot, celery, pineapple, lemon, basil, ½ tsp coconut or linseed oil (Cold-pressed oil is alkaline. It changes the property of all the juices.)
Memory loss: Pomegranate, beet, grapes, 1 tsp coconut oil. There's another thing people suffering from memory loss can do—gargle with coconut oil. Take 1 tsp oil first thing in the morning, roll it around your mouth for at least 15 minutes, pulling the oil inwards and outwards towards your teeth. This will release ketones and you will definitely see positive changes.

Salads

SHILPA'S MANTRA

Through experience and my quest for knowledge I have learnt that a balanced diet must consist of 20 per cent raw food, and ideally be consumed before 4 p.m. Its advantages include being potent in minerals, fibre and less sodium, helping in water retention, aiding weight loss and being beneficial in osteoporosis, kidney disease and type 2 diabetes. It's not recommended for people with IDS and chronic gut issues. Some studies claim that a raw-food diet can clear headaches and allergies too. So we don't need to go to extremes; adding these super nutritious salads to your diet will also go a long way. My advice: Make sure you clean your veggies and salads thoroughly.

Halloumi and Grape Salad ✿

Halloumi cheese is easily available in India now. It tastes almost like paneer; it's just a bit harder. Halloumi is made from either goat's milk or sheep's milk and has low lactose content. That makes it one of the healthiest cheeses around. The grapes balance out the milky flavour of the halloumi and give the salad a sharp citrusy flavour. This salad leaves you refreshed because it won't give you the feeling that you've overeaten.

Serves: 2
Nutritional value:
727 kcal (Carbs: 28 g,
Protein: 30 g, Fats: 55 g)

For the dressing:
4 tbsp olive oil
1 tbsp lemon juice
1 tsp honey
Salt and black pepper
powder, to taste
1 tsp chopped fresh thyme
or dill

1. To make the dressing, mix together the olive oil, lemon juice and honey in a bowl. Season with salt and pepper. Stir in the thyme or dill and set aside.

2. Toss together the salad leaves, the green grapes and cranberries, then transfer to a large serving plate.

3. Thinly slice the halloumi cheese. Heat the oil in a non-stick pan. Add the cheese and grill briefly until it turns golden on the underside. Turn the cheese with a metal spatula and cook the other side.

For the salad:
150 g mixed green salad leaves and steamed spinach
75 g seedless green grapes
1 tbsp cranberries
250 g Halloumi cheese
1 tbsp olive oil
A few fresh mint leaves, to garnish

4. Arrange the warm cheese pieces over the salad. Pour the dressing over the salad and garnish with mint leaves. Serve immediately.

SHILPA'S SECRET: If the cheese goes cold before it is served, it will become rubbery. Also, if you're unable to get halloumi, you can substitute it with paneer.

Asparagus and Orange Salad ✿

Like pumpkin, asparagus is also a great diuretic. I was introduced it to by a former trainer a long time ago. I wanted to look flat and not bloated for a song I was shooting with my sister, Shamita, the next day. My trainer suggested I have asparagus and the effect was instant. Soups and salads with asparagus work brilliantly when you want to shed water weight.

Serves: 2
Nutritional value:
334 kcal (Carbs: 61 g,
Protein: 0 g, Fats: 10 g)

225 g asparagus,
trimmed and cut into
2-inch pieces
2 large oranges
2 ripe tomatoes, cut into
eighths
50 g romaine lettuce
leaves, shredded
2 tbsp extra virgin
olive oil
½ tsp balsamic vinegar
Salt and black pepper
powder, to taste
Goat's cheese for garnish

1. Cook the asparagus in lightly salted, boiling water for 3–4 minutes until it becomes just tender. Drain and refresh under cold water. Set aside.

2. Zest half an orange and reserve. Peel both oranges and cut into segments, leaving the membrane behind. Squeeze out the juice from the membrane and reserve the juice.

3. Put the asparagus pieces, orange segments, tomatoes and lettuce into a salad bowl. Mix together the olive oil and balsamic vinegar and add 1 tbsp of the reserved orange juice and ½ tsp of the orange zest, whisking well to combine. Season with a little salt and plenty of black pepper. Just before serving, pour the dressing over the salad and toss gently to coat. Garnish with goat's cheese.

SHILPA'S SECRET: I like to do a mix of white and green asparagus. It looks so pretty and it will make your tummy look flat the next day.

Million-Dollar Salad ✌

I call this the Million-Dollar Salad because you will look like a million bucks if you start eating it before dinner, at around 5.30 p.m., for a week.

Serves: 1
Nutritional value: 194 kcal
(Carbs: 14 g, Protein: 0 g,
Fats: 12 g)
Dressing: 181 kcal
(Carbs: 10 g, Protein: 20 g,
Fats: 14 g)

For the salad:
1 bunch baby spinach,
chopped, or regular
spinach, blanched or
steamed
1 cucumber, chopped
1 small iceberg lettuce,
shredded
1 head broccoli, separated
into florets and steamed
4–5 cherry tomatoes
1 cup shredded Chinese
cabbage
1 tsp flaxseeds

1. Whisk together the ingredients for the dressing and keep aside.

2. In a bowl, mix together all the ingredients for the salad and toss with the dressing. Serve immediately.

1 tsp cranberries
1 tsp roasted pumpkin
seeds
Salt and black pepper
powder, to taste

For the dressing:
2 tsp olive oil
½ lemon, squeezed
A pinch of cayenne pepper
A pinch of black pepper
powder
A pinch of sea salt
A pinch of cumin powder
5 tbsp buttermilk made
from skimmed milk

SHILPA'S SECRET: If you eat eggs, add two poached eggs or a boiled egg on top.

Chickpea and Sweet Potato Chaat ▶

This is my take on the chaat that we all love. Chickpeas and potatoes are a combination that can never go wrong. For this salad, I've cut out all the fattening stuff and kept it clean and healthy, but still tasty. You can have this salad hot or cold.

Serves: 2
Nutritional value:
583 kcal (Carbs: 85 g,
Protein: 27 g, Fats: 15 g)

For the salad:
¾ cups soaked and boiled chickpeas
2 medium sweet potatoes, steamed and peeled
Microgreen strands (optional)

For the dressing:
5 tbsp curd
2 finely chopped green chillies
1 tsp jaggery sugar
¾ tsp dry mango powder
1 tsp chaat masala
½ tsp rock salt
½ tsp jeera powder

1. Mix the chickpeas, sweet potatoes and microgreens. Keep aside.
2. Mix the dressing ingredients in a bowl.
3. Add the dressing to the salad mix.

2 tsp mint leaves, finely chopped
½ tsp lemon juice
2 tbsp coriander, chopped finely

For the glaze (optional):
1 tbsp olive oil

For the garnish:
1½ tbsp roasted sesame seeds
1 tbsp flax seeds
2 tbsp pomegranate seeds

4. Mix it well.
5. Optional: Add the olive oil to the salad for a shine.
6. Garnish and serve.

Raw Jowar Salad 🌱

I love this recipe for two reasons: it's simple and so, so healthy. I like to keep things simple while cooking and don't use a lot of ingredients to make something good. Many of us tend to over-condiment food, but some things are best left the way nature intended us to have them. Since jowar is available only in winter, make the most of it during the cold months.

Serves: 1
Nutritional value:
46 kcal (Carbs: 7 g,
Protein: 0 g, Fats: 2 g)

1 cup raw sorghum
Salt and black pepper
powder, to taste
¼ cup pomegranate seeds
½ tsp ghee or butter
(optional)

1. Season the sorghum with salt and pepper. Add the ghee or butter if you like. Top with pomegranate seeds and serve.

Pumpkin and Bell Pepper Salad 🌱

I'm sure by now you know how much I love pumpkin. In this salad, it adds sweetness to the crunch of the bell peppers. This is a colourful salad that looks pretty served on any table.

Serves: 2
Nutritional value:
494 kcal (Carbs: 36 g,
Protein: 20 g, Fats: 30 g)

For the salad:
300 g roasted yellow
pumpkin, diced
2 tsp olive oil
Salt and black pepper
powder, to taste
½ tsp cumin seeds
2 sprigs coriander,
chopped
½ red bell pepper,
julienned
½ yellow bell pepper,
julienned

1. Whisk together all the ingredients for the dressing in a large bowl.

A few rocket leaves
½ red onion, julienned
100 g feta cheese or
paneer, crumbled
A few roasted pine nuts

For the dressing:
½ tsp vinegar
2 garlic cloves, grated
1 tsp honey
2 tsp lemon juice
Salt and black pepper
powder, to taste

2. Now add the ingredients for the salad and toss gently to coat them with the dressing.

3. Season as per taste and serve.

SHILPA'S MANTRA

My favourite alkaline foods are fig, potato, avocado, fresh lemon, tomato, carrot and green beans. Potatoes get a bad reputation because everyone believes they're fattening. But when you boil potatoes, their glycaemic index drops and the starch is eliminated. Pour some hemp oil or linseed oil over the boiled potatoes, add some chopped fresh herbs (parsley, thyme, dill, oregano) and season with salt, black pepper powder and paprika. Make sure you don't overcook them and add the seasonings while you're eating. They are a very alkaline vegetable, a wholesome food that we must make part of our diet.

Poached Eggs and Chickpeas

A hearty, protein-packed salad that will satiate your hunger pangs any time of the day—breakfast, lunch or dinner—this one is a no-brainer! Vegetarians can use grilled paneer or slabs of Halloumi instead of eggs. This is the salad I turn to when I want a light but filling meal at night or if I've just come back from a holiday (with 'holiday weight') and need to get back into shape!

Serves: 2–4
Nutritional Value: 291 kcal (Carbs: 47 g, Proteins: 10 g, Fats: 7 g)

For the chickpeas:
1 tbsp vegetable or coconut or olive oil
1 tbsp garlic paste
2 small spring onions or red or white onions
½ tsp cumin powder
½ tsp coriander powder
¼ tsp turmeric powder
½ green chilli
½ tsp cayenne pepper
½ yellow bell pepper
1½ tomatoes
1 tbsp salt
1½ cup soaked and boiled chickpeas
2–3 tbsp freshly chopped coriander

1. To make the chickpeas, heat the oil in a large pan. Add the garlic paste and cook over medium heat until it is golden brown. Now add the spring onions and sauté until browned. Next add the powdered spices and mix well. Add a little water, the yellow bell pepper and tomatoes and the boiled chickpeas. Mix well. Add salt to taste, and the coriander. Keep aside.

2. For the egg, boil 500 ml water in a large pan. Add the vinegar. Take 2 small stainless steel or silicon moulds and grease them with a drop of oil. Break the eggs into the bowls, and carefully place the bowls into the pan of boiling water with tongs. Cover the pan with a lid and reduce the flame to medium. Cook the eggs for 3–4 minutes, until you see a white layer form on the eggs. Remove the bowls of eggs from the pan and let them cool for a few minutes. Using a sharp knife, loosen the eggs from the moulds.

For the poached eggs:
500 ml water
2 eggs
1 tsp vinegar
Salt, to taste
Cayenne pepper, to taste
Black pepper powder, to
taste

3. To serve, put the chickpeas in a serving bowl and then gently place the eggs in the centre. Garnish the eggs with salt, cayenne pepper, black pepper and chopped coriander.

Starters

Dahi Bhalla ✌

I have great memories of having dahi bhalla as a child. My mother made it almost every time she entertained and the guests devoured it. No dahi bhalla has ever matched my mother's. Her bhallas were far airier, softer and not heavy at all. She also garnished the dahi so beautifully; it was almost like a rangoli, with chilli and cumin powders and coriander leaves.

You'll need to leave the batter overnight to rise, so prepare it the day before you want to serve this.

Makes: 10–12 bhallas
Nutritional value:
2854 kcal (Carbs: 506 g,
Protein: 122 g, Fats: 38 g)

For the bhalla:
2 cups urad dal, soaked
2-inch ginger, roughly
chopped
2 green chilli, finely
chopped
Salt, to taste
Oil, for deep frying

1. Boil the dates, tamarind pulp and jaggery in water. Then strain and reserve the tamarind chutney.

2. Grind all the ingredients for the bhalla and keep overnight in a warm place. Put the mixture in a deep container because the batter will rise. When you're ready to fry the bhallas, scoop out a bit of the batter with a big tablespoon and drop it into hot oil and deep fry in a wok. You can fry 4–5 vadas at a time. Once they're golden brown, remove from the oil and immediately put in a bowl of ice water. Squeeze out the excess water and set aside.

For the dahi:
750 g plain curd,
sweetened with 6 tbsp
brown sugar
½ tsp cumin powder
½ tsp dry coriander
powder
½ tsp red chilli powder

For the chutney:
4 dates
3 tbsp tamarind pulp
75 g jaggery
500 ml water

3. To serve, place the bhalla in a bowl and pour the sweetened curd over it. Sprinkle the cumin, dry coriander and chilli powders and pour a few teaspoons of the tamarind chutney.

Walnut and Garlic Dip 🌿

I love all dips. They're great when you have friends over and kids enjoy them too. This particular one is my favourite because it has walnut in it. A nutty dip is high in protein. This one has always got me compliments.

Makes: 1 bowl
Nutritional value:
898 kcal (Carbs: 27 g,
Protein: 13 g, Fats: 82 g)

2½–inch slices of 5-grain bread
4 tbsp milk
1¼ cups shelled walnuts
4 garlic cloves, chopped
5 tbsp extra virgin olive oil
1–2 tbsp walnut oil (optional)
Juice of 1 lemon
Salt and black pepper powder, to taste
Walnut or olive oil, for drizzling
Paprika, for dusting (optional)

1. Remove the crust from the bread, and soak the slices in milk for 5 minutes. Then process them along with the walnuts and chopped garlic in a food processor or blender to a coarse paste.

2. With the motor still running, add the olive oil to the paste in a steady stream, until the mixture forms a smooth, thick sauce. Blend in the walnut oil, if you're using it.

3. Scoop the sauce into a bowl and add lemon juice to taste, season with salt and pepper and mix well.

4. When serving, drizzle a little more walnut or olive oil over the dip, and dust lightly with the paprika, if you wish to.

Pumpkin, Peanut Butter and Oat Bars ✿

A lot of working women ask me how they can lose weight. The best way to do that is to eat homemade food instead of ordering in. Munch on these delicious bars a few times a week and carry them with you to work or even when you're travelling on long journeys. That way you'll eat right.

Makes: 8–10
Nutritional value:
1983 kcal (Carbs: 295 g,
Protein: 77 g, Fats: 55 g)

½ cup shredded pumpkin
5 tbsp honey or agave
syrup or 4 tbsp coconut
sugar or jaggery
4 tbsp unsweetened
peanut butter
3 tbsp raisins (optional)
3 tbsp chopped pistachios
(optional)
¼ tsp sea salt
½ tsp vanilla extract
¼ tsp baking soda
¼ tsp ginger powder
2½ cups oats

1. Preheat the oven to 180°C.
2. Take all the ingredients except the oats in a large bowl and combine thoroughly. Now add the oats, making sure they're coated well.
3. Layer an 8x8" or 9x9" cake tray with parchment paper. Pour in the wet mixture and bake for 25 minutes.
4. Once they're cooled, cut them into bars.

SHILPA'S SECRET: Store these bars in an airtight container and eat whenever you please. They'll keep for at least a couple of weeks. These are great for picnics and travels, or even a tea-time snack.

SHILPA'S TIP: If you're allergic to peanuts, use almond butter.

All-Natural Nutrition Bar 🌿 ▶

In this day and age when you get something natural you should pounce on it! With this satiating energy bar you don't have to label-read—it is precisely what it claims to be: All Natural. The best part about this is that you can make it at home in minutes, and it is great for snacking.

Nutritional value:
2758 kcal
(Carbs: 240 g, Protein: 85 g, Fats: 162 g)

1½ cup oats
½ cup almonds
3 tbsp flax seed
¼ tsp nutmeg powder
¼ tsp cinnamon powder
2 tbsp honey
1 cup peanut butter
1 tsp vanilla essence
½ tsp almond essence
½ tsp salt
2 tsp coconut oil, plus extra for greasing

1. In a pan over a medium flame, dry roast the oats for 5 minutes.
2. Now, in mixer grinder, add the roasted oats, almonds, flax seed, nutmeg powder, cinnamon powder and blend until you get a coarse mixture.
3. Transfer the mixture to a large bowl and add honey, peanut butter, vanilla essence, almond essence, salt, coconut oil and mix well.
4. Grease a large tray with coconut oil and transfer the mixture to the tray.
5. Flatten the mixture, pressing down firmly.
6. Keep the tray in the freezer for an hour. Take it out and cut it into rectangles. Your no-bake nutrition bar is ready.

SHILPA'S TIP: If you don't like peanut butter, you can substitute it with almond butter or dates.

You can even add a mashed banana into it for added flavour. The drawback is that it only keeps for 2 days in the fridge, so you must consume it within that time.

Zucchini Fritters with Chilli Jam ✿

This is a dish I make on Sundays when I allow myself fried food.

Makes: 12
Nutritional value:
Chilli jam: 310 kcal
(Carbs: 80 g, Protein: 4 g,
Fats: 225 g)
Fritters: 680 kcal
(Carbs: 40 g, Protein:
22 g, Fats: 47 g)

For the chilli jam:
5 tbsp olive oil
4 large onions, diced
4 garlic cloves, chopped
1–2 fresh red chillies,
deseeded and sliced
1 tbsp dark brown soft
sugar or jaggery

1. To make the chilli jam, heat the oil in a large, heavy pan, and then add the onions and the garlic. Reduce the heat to low and cook for 20 minutes, stirring frequently, until the onions are very soft.

2. Remove the pan from the stove and leave the onion mixture to cool. Transfer it to a food processor or blender. Add the chillies and sugar and process until smooth, and then return the mixture to the pan. Cook over low heat for 10 minutes, stirring frequently until the liquid has evaporated and the mixture has the consistency of jam. Cool slightly.

3. To make the fritters, squeeze the courgettes in a dishtowel to remove any excess liquid, then combine with the grated Parmesan, eggs and potato or breadcrumbs and season with salt and pepper.

4. Pour in enough oil to cover the base of a large frying pan and heat. Add 2 tbsp of the courgette mixture for each fritter and cook three fritters at a time. Cook for 2–3 minutes on each side until they turn golden. Drain on paper towels to get rid of the excess oil and serve warm with a spoonful of the chilli jam.

For the fritters:
450 g coarsely grated
courgettes (zucchini)
50 g freshly grated
Parmesan
2 eggs, beaten
4 tbsp plain breadcrumbs
or 1 sweet potato
Salt and black pepper
powder, to taste
Vegetable oil, for frying
1 red chilli, sliced

SHILPA'S SECRET: Stored in an airtight jar in the refrigerator, the chilli jam will keep for up to one week. Chilli jam is hot, sweet and sticky—like thick chutney. It adds a delicious piquancy to these light zucchini fritters, which are a popular dish in my home.

VARIATION: If you don't like chillies or you are short of time, serve the fritters with an easy-to-make dip. Chop a bunch of spring onions (scallions) and stir them into 150 ml sour cream or simply combine finely chopped fresh herbs with a bowl of good-quality mayonnaise.

Spicy Koftas

This is a starter that my in-laws love. Whenever they visit us, I make it a point to make my special koftas. It's a great favourite at parties as well; they fill you up just enough until dinner arrives.

Makes: 20–25
Nutritional value:
312 kcal (Carbs: 34 g,
Protein: 8 g, Fats: 16 g)

450 g minced lamb
2 tbsp ginger paste
2 tbsp finely chopped garlic
4 green chillies, finely chopped
1 small onion, finely chopped
1 egg
½ tsp turmeric powder
1 tsp garam masala
2 cups chopped coriander leaves
4–6 mint leaves, chopped
175 g potato, boiled
Salt, to taste,
1 tbsp lemon juice
2 tbsp ghee
Oil, to fry

1. Place the meat in a large bowl with the ginger, garlic, chillies, onion, egg, turmeric powder, garam masala, coriander and mint. Grate the potato into the bowl, and season with salt. Add ghee and lemon juice. Mix well to form a soft dough.

2. Using your fingers, shape the kofta mixture into portions about the size of golf balls, and flatten them. You should be able to make 20–25 koftas. Place the koftas in a single layer on a baking sheet or large tray, cover with a clean dishtowel and leave at room temperature for about 25 minutes.

3. Heat oil in a large, heavy frying pan to medium-hot. Deep fry the koftas, in batches, until they are golden brown in colour. Drain the koftas on paper towels and keep warm in a low oven. Alternatively, you can also bake them for 35–40 minutes at 190°C. Transfer to a platter and serve.

SHILPA'S SECRET: Leftover koftas can be roughly chopped and packed into pita bread spread with chutney or relish for a quick, easy and delicious snack. They can also be used in a tomato gravy and paired with spaghetti for children and grown-ups. My son loves this.

VARIATION: Although lamb is traditionally used for making koftas, they are also delicious made with lean minced chicken. Vegetarians can substitute the lamb with soya.

Chicken Bitki

Bitkis are a great serving option for nonvegetarians. They're juicy and perfect as a filling starter. Like many of my dishes, this one can be used the next day too. Well, that's the middle-class girl in me.

Makes: 12
Nutritional value:
770 kcal (Carbs: 33 g,
Protein: 65 g, Fats: 13 g)

1 tbsp butter, melted
115 g flat mushrooms,
finely chopped
1 cup fresh white
breadcrumbs
350 g skinless chicken
breast portions, minced or
finely chopped
2 eggs, separated
¼ tsp grated nutmeg
2 tbsp plain (all-purpose)
flour
3 tbsp vegetable oil
Salt and black pepper
powder, to taste
Salad leaves and grated
pickled beetroot to serve

1. Melt the butter in a pan and cook the mushrooms for about five minutes, until they are soft and the juices have evaporated. Leave to cool.

2. Mix together the mushrooms, breadcrumbs, chicken, egg yolks and nutmeg in a bowl and season with salt and pepper.

3. Take the egg whites in a clean, dry, grease-free bowl and whisk until stiff. Gently stir half the whites into the chicken mixture to slacken it, then fold in the remainder with a rubber spatula or metal spoon.

4. Shape the mixture into 12 even-sized bitkis, about 3 inches long and 1 inch wide. Spread out the flour on a shallow plate. Roll the bitkis in the flour to coat.

5. Heat the oil in a large, heavy frying pan. Fry the bitkis over medium heat for about 10 minutes, turning occasionally until they are golden brown and cooked through. Serve hot with salad leaves and grated pickled beetroot.

VARIATION: Vegetarians can use paneer or minced soya instead of chicken.

Lemon and Coconut Dal Dip ✿

This dip is basically dal that's not runny. This too is an unusual dip and a hot favourite every time I serve it at my in-laws' home in London.

*Makes: 2 bowls, for
8–10 people
Nutritional value:
1657 cal (Carbs: 42 g,
Protein: 46 g, Fats: 145 g)*

*⅔ cup red lentils
1 cup water
Juice of 1 lemon
Handful of fresh
coriander leaves
¼ cup sliced almonds
Salt and black pepper
powder, to taste
1 cup coconut cream*

*For the curry paste:
2 tbsp vegetable or
coconut oil
2-inch piece fresh ginger,
finely chopped*

1. To make the curry paste, heat the oil in a large, shallow pan. Add the ginger, onion, garlic, chillies, cumin seeds and garam masala. Cook over medium heat, stirring occasionally, for about 5 minutes, until the onion has softened but not browned. Blend this mixture to make the curry paste.

2. Stir the lentils, water and curry paste into the pan. Bring to a boil, then reduce the heat to low. Cover the pan and simmer gently for 15–20 minutes, stirring occasionally, until the lentils are just tender but have not yet broken.

3. Bring to a boil and cook, uncovered, for 15–20 minutes, until the mixture is thick and pulpy. Remove the pan from the heat, stir in the lemon juice and add the coriander leaves. Season with salt and pepper.

4. Heat a large, heavy frying pan and dry-roast the sliced almonds for 1–2 minutes on each side, until golden brown. Stir about three-quarters of the toasted almonds into the dal. Reserve the remainder for the garnish.

1 onion, finely chopped
2 garlic cloves, finely
chopped
2 small fresh red chillies,
deseeded
1 tsp cumin seeds
1 tbsp garam masala

5. Transfer the dal to a serving bowl, swirl in the coconut cream. Sprinkle the reserved almonds on top and serve warm.

VARIATION: Try making this dal with yellow split peas as well. They take longer to cook and a little extra water has to be added, but the result is equally tasty and protein rich.

Serve with lavash or pita bread or even just carrots and cucumber.

Avocado Salsa ✿

Avocado is actually a fruit and not a vegetable like most people think it is. It's alkaline so my body feels great after I have it. It has good fats that do your body good.

Makes: 1 bowl, for 4–5 people
Nutritional value:
789 kcal (Carbs: 43 g, Protein: 8 g, Fats: 65 g)

2 large ripe avocados
1 small red onion, very finely chopped
1 fresh red or green chilli, seeded and finely minced
1 garlic clove, crushed (optional)
Zest of ½ lime
Juice of 1–1½ limes
Pinch of brown sugar
2 big tomatoes, seeded and chopped
2 tbsp coarsely chopped fresh coriander leaves

1. Halve, stone (pit) and peel the avocados. Set half the flesh aside and coarsely mash the remainder in a bowl using a fork.

2. Add the onion, chilli, garlic, lime zest, juice of 1 lime, sugar, tomatoes and coriander leaves. Add the ground cumin, and season with more lime juice if required. Stir in the olive oil.

3. Dice the remaining avocado and stir into the salsa, then cover and let it stand for 15 minutes so that the flavour develops. Stir in the sour cream, if you're using it. Serve immediately with lime wedges dipped in sea salt and fresh coriander sprigs.

½–1 tsp cumin powder
1–2 tbsp sour cream
(optional)
Salt and black pepper
powder, to taste
1 tbsp olive oil
Lime wedges dipped
in sea salt and a few
coriander sprigs, to
garnish

SHILPA'S SECRET: Leaving some of the avocados in chunks adds a slightly different texture, but if you like a smoother salsa, mash all the avocado together. Hard avocados will soften in a few seconds in a microwave. Check frequently until you get the softness you desire.

Courgette and Aubergine Crisps ✿

If you feel guilty about gorging on potato crisps, these vegetable crisps are a good alternative. These are very tasty and simple to make. They're a good way of feeding your family vegetables, adding the perfect crunch to a simple meal of dal and chawal. I'd rather have these crisps than papad. Once fried, put them on a some paper towels to drain the excess oil. You can serve these as a starter, or as a side dish with dal and rice.

Serves: 2
Nutritional value:
276 kcal (Carbs: 47 g,
Protein: 4 g, Fats: 8 g)

½ tsp coriander powder
½ tsp turmeric
1 tsp red chilli powder
1 tsp dry ginger powder
Salt and black pepper powder, to taste
1 medium courgette, thinly sliced into rounds
1 medium aubergine, sliced into rounds
2 tbsp semolina
Coconut or vegetable oil, for frying

1. Mix the dry ingredients into a masala.
2. Coat the courgette and aubergine slices with the masala.
3. Next, coat them with semolina, so the fritters are crispy after frying.
4. In a shallow pan, heat the oil and fry the fritters, a few at a time. Once they're golden, remove them from the oil and drain on paper towels. Serve hot.

SHILPA'S TIP: If you don't want to fry them, you can drizzle a tablespoon of vegetable oil over them and bake them at 180°C for 30 minutes. They are ready to serve once they've browned.

Spicy Hummus ✿

Hummus is a great source of protein. We eat it while watching movies at home instead of popcorn. I like a bit of kick in my food, hence the spice in this recipe.

Serves: 4
Nutritional value:
464 kcal (Carbs: 61 g,
Protein: 19 g, Fats: 16 g)

1 bowl chickpeas, soaked overnight and boiled
2 tbsp tahini
2 tbsp olive oil
3 garlic bulbs, halved and roasted at 180 °C for 20 minutes
Salt and black pepper powder, to taste
1 red chilli, finely chopped
Water, to blend
1 tsp each flaxseeds and chia seeds, to garnish

1. Blend all the ingredients with half the seeds in a mixer. Garnish with remaining flax and chia seeds and serve chilled or at room temperature with lavash or carrot, cucumber or radish crudités.

Bunt Bombs ▶

We Shettys belong to the Bunt community of Mangalore and this dish is quite popular in 'my clan'. It is served usually when the men sit to drink, but I've cooked it as part of every meal, including breakfast for my son. This dish takes away most of the egg flavour and has a nice spicy touch to it. Don't underestimate the taste of this dish because of its simplicity. I assure you it will burst like a bomb full of flavours in your mouth, satiating your hunger and tingling your taste buds. I have these eggs for breakfast, as an evening snack or even serve it to guests as a starter.

Serves: 4
Nutritional value:
325 kcal (Carbs: 0 g,
Protein: 24 g, Fats: 29 g)

4 eggs, boiled for
8 minutes and shelled
1 tsp oil or ghee
¾ tsp chilli powder
½ tsp turmeric powder
½ tsp black pepper powder
1 sprig of coriander
(optional)
Salt, to taste

1. Make four vertical slits on each egg. Set aside.
2. Heat oil and add all the spices and salt. After a minute, add the eggs and gently mix. Remove from heat after 30 seconds and serve hot, garnished with coriander.

Fried Idli 🌿

Idlis can be made in so many ways and the best part is that the leftover idlis can always be used to cook a completely different dish. Idlis are gluten-free and fried idlis are a good break from the way we usually eat them, with sambhar and chutney.

Serves: 2
Nutritional value:
100 kcal (Carbs: 20 g, Protein: 0 g, Fats: 5 g)

1 tbsp butter, ghee or oil (I prefer ghee)
¾ tsp chilli powder
½ tsp turmeric powder
½ tsp black pepper powder
¼ tsp coriander powder
¼ tsp cumin powder
4 idlis, cut into 4 pieces

1. Heat the butter in a pan on medium heat and add all the spices.
2. Add the idlis and continue to stir-fry on medium heat till they are brown on all sides. Remove from heat after 30 seconds and serve hot.

Polenta Starter ✌

I'm fond of polenta because it's low in carbs and since it's gluten-free, it's good for people with coeliac disease. My husband Raj used to suffer from many allergies. I remember serving him a lot of polenta. Polenta is not tasteless like couscous, so he enjoyed it.

Serves: 2
Nutritional value:
85 kcal (Carbs: 17 g,
Protein: 3 g, Fats: 1 g)

1 cup polenta
1 tomato, sliced and roasted
2–3 garlic cloves, mashed
Salt and black pepper powder, to taste
A few basil leaves, chopped
Olive oil, to drizzle

1. Cook the polenta and top it with the roasted tomato and garlic.
2. Top with chopped basil and pepper. Drizzle a little olive oil on it and serve.

SHILPA'S TIP: 'Keep it simple!' Less is more.

Lotus Root and Potato Cutlet ❧

Lotus root is known to improve digestion, reduce cholesterol, lower blood pressure and boost our immune systems. I love all dishes that have them; they're so tasty! This one is a different starter that combines potato with lotus root in a cutlet that's crisp even though it's not fried.

Serves: 3
Nutritional value:
835 kcal (Carbs: 155 g,
Protein: 20 g, Fats: 15 g)

500 g lotus root
2 tsp oil
½ tsp black pepper
powder
1 tbsp chaat masala
(optional)
½ red chilli, chopped
1 tsp honey
2 large potatoes, boiled
and mashed
A bit of jaggery
Salt, to taste
½ tsp mint powder or
fresh mint leaves
2 red or green chillies,
deseeded and finely
chopped
3 tbsp breadcrumbs
Chilli flakes, to taste

1. Blanch the lotus root first.

2. In a pan, stir-fry the lotus root with 1 tsp oil, the pepper powder, red chilli, honey and chaat masala. Set aside.

3. In a large bowl, combine the mashed potatoes, jaggery, salt, mint powder, chopped chillies and breadcrumbs. The breadcrumbs will hold the mixture together.

4. Mash the lotus root and mix with the potato mixture and make into tikkis.

5. On low heat, heat the remaining 1 tsp oil and gently place the tikkis in it. Let them cook till one side is medium brown and turn over. Remove from heat when both sides are done, season with chilli flakes and serve with mint chutney.

Bhindi Kurkure ✤

This is a signature dish in my house. It can be served with both Indian as well as continental food. Okra is a vegetable that's underestimated and I hope with this recipe I can get more people to eat it. This is the only form in which my sister eats okra. I love this dish, even though it is fried. It's good to let go sometimes and indulge!

Serves: 2
Nutritional value:
172 kcal (Carbs: 40 g,
Protein: 3 g, Fats: 0 g)

1 tsp cumin seeds
½ tsp carom seeds
3 small pieces of ginger
2 green chillies
4 cloves of garlic
3 tbsp gram flour
2 tbsp rice flour
½ tsp dry mango powder
½ tsp turmeric powder
½ tsp garam masala
250 g okra
Salt, to taste
Oil, to fry
Chaat masala, to taste

1. Coarsely grind the cumin seeds, carom seeds, ginger, green chillies, garlic, gram flour, rice flour, dry mango powder, turmeric powder and garam masala together and set aside.
2. Wash and dry the okra and cut them into long strips, removing all the seeds. Mix the okra and the masala. Season with salt.
3. Heat oil in a wok and fry the okra till it's crisp. Sprinkle chaat masala on top and serve it hot.

SHILPA'S SECRET: I always drain fried food in four layers of tissue, under which I have spread a newspaper. It works like magic!

Cauli-Fish and Chips ✿

This dish is my vegetarian take on a classic. Even if the dish doesn't imitate fish exactly, it does have the right light feeling, and with a squeeze of lemon on top and a dollop of tartare sauce it all feels rather convincing. As with most foods you can eat with your hands, this dish is very kid-friendly, but adults love it too.

Serves: 4
Nutritional value:
1860 kcal (Carbs: 110 g,
Protein: 73 g, Fats: 112 g)

For the cauli-fish:
2 tbsp virgin coconut oil
or extra virgin olive oil
1 onion, finely chopped
1 leek, washed, trimmed,
tops removed and finely
chopped
2 cloves of garlic, finely
chopped
1 medium cauliflower,
head and stalk trimmed
and chopped
1 courgette, grated and
excess water squeezed out
2 eggs
120 g almond flour
150 g paneer
Zest of 1 large lemon
½ tsp sea salt

1. Preheat the oven to 200°C and line two baking trays with parchment paper.

2. Heat the oil for the cauli-fish in a large frying pan, on medium-low heat. Add the onion, leek and garlic to the pan and sauté for about 15 minutes or until the onion and leek have softened.

3. Meanwhile, transfer the chopped cauliflower to a food processor and blend until the texture resembles coarse breadcrumbs. Set aside.

4. Crack the eggs into a large mixing bowl and whisk until the yolks and whites are combined. Add the sautéed vegetables, cauliflower, courgette and remaining ingredients for the cauli-fish and mix until combined.

5. Dip 2 spoons (or your hands) into hot water and shake off the excess water. Take a generous scoop of the mixture and pass it repeatedly between the spoons, turning and smoothing each side until a neat ball is formed. Place the balls on one of the baking trays.

For the potato chips:
500 g baby potatoes, cut
into quarters
2 tbsp extra virgin olive oil
Salt and black pepper
powder, to taste

For the tartare sauce:
2 tbsp capers, drained
and roughly chopped
3 tbsp chopped fresh flat-
leaf parsley
250 ml plain yoghurt
Juice of 1 lemon
Salt and black pepper
powder, to taste

To serve:
Fresh flat-leaf parsley
Lemon wedges

6. To make the potato chips, transfer the potato pieces to the second baking tray. Drizzle with the oil, season with salt and pepper and toss until they're well coated.

7. Bake the cauli-fish and potato chips simultaneously for 25–30 minutes.

8. In the meantime, roughly chop the capers and transfer them to a small mixing bowl. Add the remaining ingredients for the tartare sauce, season with salt and pepper and mix until combined.

9. Serve the cauli-fish accompanied and potato chips with the tartare sauce, parsley and lemon wedges.

Kothambirvadi ✿

Kothambirvadi is a Maharashtrian starter that my husband, a Punjabi from London, could eat every day. The love with which he enjoys this dish is why I've included it in this book.

Serves: 4
Nutritional value:
170 kcal (Carbs: 25 g,
Protein: 6 g, Fat: 5 g)

4–5 green chillies,
chopped
6–8 garlic cloves, chopped
2 tsp coriander seeds
1 tsp cumin seeds
1 small piece ginger
2 big bunches fresh
coriander, finely chopped
1½ cup chickpea flour or
gram flour
Salt, to taste
¼ tsp turmeric powder
½ tsp red chilli powder
¼ tsp baking soda
¼ tsp asafoetida
1 tsp sesame seeds, plus a
few for garnishing
Water, as needed
1 tsp oil

1. In a small blender, put the green chillies, garlic cloves, coriander seeds, cumin seeds and ginger with very little water. Blend well to make a coarse mixture. Set aside.

2. Place the coriander in a large bowl. To this, add the flour and salt. Now add the coarse mixture, turmeric and red chilli powders, baking soda, asafoetida and sesame seeds. Mix this well without using water. Once it's thoroughly combined, add a little water at a time to make a semi-stiff dough.

3. Once the dough is ready, divide it into two equal parts. Apply some oil to your hand and roll the two parts into two long rolls.

4. Steam the rolls on a greased perforated plate by placing the plate on boiling water for 20–25 minutes.

5. After they are steamed, cut the rolls into ¼-inch pieces.

6. In a non-stick pan, sauté the vadis with very little oil. Garnish with sesame seeds and serve hot.

Mains

Pizza Base ✌

I try to avoid refined flour (maida) as much as possible, so gluten-free or wheat flour is what I turn to when making pizza bases at home. It helps that gluten-free flour is available everywhere these days. The only reason the pizza base recipe is in the book is that it's better to make it at home rather than buy it at a store. And who doesn't love pizza? This way you can have it more often than you would if you used a store-bought ready-made base. I've also got my son involved in making the pizzas when I'm done with the bases. That's better than him spending hours on his iPad or watching television.

Makes: 6 6-inch pizzas
Nutritional value:
584 kcal (Carbs: 73 g,
Protein: 28 g, Fats: 20 g)

2½ cups gluten-free flour
1½ tsp baking powder
1 tsp sea salt
2 cloves garlic, crushed
1 tsp olive oil
2 eggs (1 whole and 1 egg white, beaten)
½ cup warm milk
½ cup warm water
1 tbsp chopped basil
Oregano, to taste

1. Preheat the oven to 200°C.
2. Mix all dry ingredients in a bowl for 3 minutes.
3. Add the oil, eggs, milk, water and basil and combine. Make sure the mixture is sticky, not runny.
4. Divide the mixture into 6 balls and roll them out until they are half an inch thick.
5. Bake for 8 minutes on each side.

Cauliflower Crust Pizza

This is a guilt-free crispy pizza with no gluten. Yaay! In fact, you can call this is a 'healthy pizza'!

Serves: 2
Nutritional value:
462 kcal (Carbs: 12 g,
Protein: 36 g, Fats: 30 g)

250 g cauliflower
½ cup shredded
mozzarella + 20 g for
sprinkling
¼ cup Parmesan
1 egg
½ tsp oil
3 garlic cloves, crushed
3 tbsp tomato puree
1 tbsp tomato ketchup
¼ tsp jaggery
2 tsp fresh basil leaves
1 tsp Italian herbs
A handful of rocket leaves
1 tbsp peas

1. Place the cauliflower in a food processor and blitz until it forms crumbs. Now lightly steam it and squeeze out any excess moisture.

2. Combine the cauliflower with the shredded mozzarella and Parmesan.

3. Beat in the egg and mix well to form a dough.

4. Spray or brush a baking tray with the oil. Using your hands, shape the dough into a ball before flattening it on the tray.

5. Place the base in the oven and bake at 180°C for about 15 minutes or until it's golden.

6. Mix the garlic, tomato puree, ketchup, jaggery, basil and Italian herbs to make a sauce for the pizza. Smear it on to the pizza base.

7. Top the pizza with the remaining mozzarella, rocket leaves and peas and serve.

VARIATION: Vegetarians can replace the egg with 1 tsp of vinegar and 1 tbsp arrowroot powder.

My Version of Spanish Omelette

This is my star dish and can be served as breakfast, lunch or dinner as this is a wholesome meal with carbs and protein. My recipe just has an Indian touch with chillies and turmeric. Turmeric is very good for health because it's anti-inflammatory. I like that the omelette is thick, just like a quiche.

Serves: 2
Nutritional value:
464 kcal (Carbs: 30 g,
Protein: 14 g, Fats: 32 g)

3 eggs
5 tbsp oil
Salt and black pepper
powder, to taste
½ tsp turmeric powder
½ green chilli, minced
1 sprig coriander, chopped
1 potato, parboiled and cut
into ½ cm slices lengthwise
1 onion, finely sliced
¼ tsp cayenne pepper
(optional)

1. Break the eggs into a bowl and beat with a fork. Season with salt and pepper. Add turmeric powder, green chilli and coriander.

2. Heat the oil in a frying pan and add the onions. Once they have browned, take them out. Add the precooked potatoes to the same pan and fry for 5–7 minutes, until crispy. Drain out all the excess oil, and add the onions back into the pan.

3. Pour the egg mixture over the onion and potato. Cook over medium heat for 5–7 minutes. Top with a dash of cayenne pepper and serve hot.

SHILPA'S SECRET: Add grated Cheddar cheese. Don't mix this with other carbs. Have it with a side of steamed vegetables instead. Even the kids will love it.

Usha Rani's (Secret Gobi) Baingan Bharta 🌱

My mother-in-law makes very good baingan bharta. Her secret ingredient is cauliflower, which I learnt recently, when I asked her about it, after sampling her delicious dish for years and wondering why her bharta tastes so good! Here's why:

Serves: 2
Nutritional value:
370 kcal (Carbs: 80 g, Protein: 10 g, Fats: 10 g)

2 tbsp vegetable oil, plus more for grilling
2 aubergines
3 big onions, chopped
2–3 cloves garlic
1 cup grated cauliflower
2 large tomatoes, chopped
1 tbsp tomato puree
½ tsp paprika powder
1 green chilli, chopped
1 tsp salt

1. Brush the aubergines with a little oil and grill at 190°C for 30 minutes, turning them halfway. If you're not comfortable using the grill, you can do it over an open flame on your cooktop. Set aside.

2. Heat the vegetable oil in a pan over medium heat and sauté the onions till they're golden brown. Then add the garlic along with the grated cauliflower. Let it cook for a few minutes.

3. Add the chopped tomatoes and cook till all the water has dried up. Mix in the tomato puree and add the grilled aubergine.

4. Season with paprika powder, green chilli and salt.

SHILPA'S SECRET: The quantity of onions should be in proportion to the aubergine.

Tauthe Curry 🌿

I have grown up eating this dish. Tauthe is the Tulu name for the oval cucumber that has yellow and green stripes. It is available with most vegetable vendors. This dish is made throughout the year in Mangalore, particularly in the summers as it is cooling. The cucumber keeps for a long time without spoiling. Eat it with brown rice and a spoonful of ghee.

Serves: 4–6
Nutritional value:
819 kcal (Carbs: 30 g,
Protein: 6 g, Fats: 75 g)

1 small red cucumber,
cut into medium pieces
without removing the skin

For the masala:
½ coconut, grated
8–10 red chillies, roasted
½ tsp cumin seeds, roasted
1 tsp coriander seeds,
roasted
3 garlic cloves
½ tsp turmeric powder

1. Grind the coconut, chillies, cumin seeds, roasted coriander seeds, garlic and turmeric powder to a rough paste.

2. Boil the cucumber in 3–4 cups of water, with the tamarind water, jaggery and salt. When it's cooked, add the ground masala and cook for some more time.

3. Heat oil in a vessel and add the ingredients for the seasoning one after the other. When the garlic turns red, pour the seasoning over the masala and cover. Simmer for 5 minutes. Serve hot with brown rice.

A lime-sized ball of tamarind, soaked in water
A lime-sized piece of jaggery
Salt, to taste

For the seasoning:
2 tbsp oil (coconut)
1 tsp mustard seeds
5 curry leaves
½ tsp urad dal
5–6 garlic cloves, crushed

SHILPA'S SECRET: Soak tamarind in ½ cup of warm water for 10 minutes. Squeeze out the pulp and add jaggery to it.

Roasting the chillies, cumin and coriander seeds brings out their flavours.

Paneer and Mushroom Bhurji 🌿

Usually, paneer bhurji is made without mushrooms. But mushrooms make the dish heavier and more filling. I have used this as stuffing for a sandwich the next day. I slather on some butter on my bread or tortilla roll, fill in the bhurji and take it along to my morning meetings.

Serves: 2
Nutritional value:
540 kcal (Carbs: 12 g,
Protein: 33 g, Fats: 40 g)

2 tbsp oil
½ tsp grated ginger
1 large onion, chopped
2 chillies, deseeded and chopped
7–8 large mushrooms, chopped
1 tsp garam masala
½ tsp cumin powder
½ tsp coriander powder
½ tsp turmeric powder
Salt to taste
250 g paneer, crumbled
A few sprigs of coriander

1. Heat the oil in a pan on medium heat. After a minute, add the ginger and chopped onions and stir-fry them.

2. Now add the chillies and mushrooms along with the spices and mix well.

3. Add the paneer and combine well. Garnish with coriander leaves and serve hot.

VARIATION: If you're a nonvegetarian who enjoys eating paneer, you can break an egg into this and make it an egg and paneer bhurji. The egg will bind the bhurji together, whereas paneer tends to crumble. This adds more protein to your food.

Non-Saag Saag 🌿

This is a dish we serve when sarson ka saag is not available, with makki di roti and white butter on the side. So far no one has realized that this dish doesn't contain any saag! Pureeing spinach, fenugreek and broccoli give you the same texture as saag.

Serves: 1
Nutritional value:
197 kcal (Carbs: 27 g,
Protein: 11 g, Fats: 5 g)

1 bunch spinach, chopped
½ bunch fenugreek,
chopped
250 g broccoli
1 onion, chopped
2 tomatoes, chopped
2 green chillies, minced
1 tsp ghee or 1 tbsp
mustard oil
5 cloves garlic, minced
1 pinch asafoetida
2 Kashmiri red chillies
(break into 4 pieces)
½ tsp salt
½ tbsp turmeric powder
1 cup water
½ cup water with 1 tsp
cornflour (optional)

1. In a pressure cooker, cook all the chopped vegetables in 1 cup of water. After 5 whistles, remove the cooker from the heat and mash the vegetables coarsely. Set aside. If you find the saag thin, add 1 tsp of cornflour mixed with water to thicken it.

2. In a frying pan, heat 1 tsp ghee and add the garlic, asafoetida, Kashmiri red chillies and turmeric powder. After a minute, add the mashed vegetables and mix well. Add salt to taste.

3. Serve with *makki di roti*, white butter and powdered jaggery.

How to Cure Fish

*This is a prep before marination. **It aims at taking out the moisture and enhances the flavour of the fish.** This marinade goes well with trout or sea bass, salmon or basa.*

For 2 5-inch pieces
Nutritional value: 20 kcal

First cure:
1 tbsp sugar
1 tbsp sea salt
Zest of half a lemon
1 tbsp black pepper powder

Marinade for steamed fish:
1 tbsp vinegar
1 tbsp tamari
2 red chillies, deseeded and sliced thinly
A few sesame seeds
2 spring onions, cut lengthwise
A knob of ginger, cut lengthwise and sliced thinly
Salt and black pepper powder, to taste

First cure
1. Mix all the ingredients and cover the fish with this marinade after taking out excess water.

Marinade for steamed fish
1. Mix all the ingredients and marinate the fish with this.

Gina's Haleem

My whole family's go-to meat is mutton, particularly on special occasions. Whether there's been a birth in the family or a death or if it's just a regular party, mutton is always served. My cousin's wife, Gina, is a fantastic cook and makes this dish regularly. She constantly entertains because her husband loves having guests over. Her haleem has been very well received over the years.

Serves: 2
Nutritional value:
4103 kcal (Carbs: 552 g,
Protein: 296 g, Fats: 79 g)

1 cup wheat, dehusked
1 cup barley, dehusked
½ cup split Bengal gram
½ cup skinless split green gram (yellow)
½ cup split red lentils
½ cup skinless black gram
3 tbsp organic ghee
5 onions, sliced
6 tbsp ginger–garlic paste
500 g boneless mutton
500 g mutton bones
1 tsp turmeric powder
Salt, to taste
3 tsp red chilli powder
½ tsp mace

1. Wash the grains and lentils thoroughly and soak overnight.

2. In a large pressure cooker, heat the ghee. Once it's hot, add the 4 onions and sauté them till they're brown. Add 4 tbsp of ginger–garlic paste and fry for a few minutes until fragrant.

3. Add the mutton to the cooker. Keep it on till it browns slightly.

4. Add the turmeric powder, salt, 2 tsp red chilli powder, mace, nutmeg, black pepper powder, coriander powder, cumin, garlic powder, ginger powder, 1 tbsp garam masala and the bay leaf. Roast the masalas on low heat for 10 minutes. Add enough water to cover the meat and pressure cook for two whistles.

5. In a second pressure cooker, place the soaked grains and dals. Add 1 tsp red chilli powder, 1 tbsp garam masala and 2 tbsp ginger–garlic paste. Add sufficient water and pressure cook for 4–5 whistles.

½ tsp nutmeg powder
1 tsp black pepper powder
2 tsp coriander powder
2 tsp cumin powder
1 tsp garlic powder
1 tsp ginger powder
2 tbsp garam masala
1 bay leaf

For the garnish:
2 tbsp chopped coriander
2 tbsp chopped mint
Juice of 1 lime
1 onion, sliced and fried
until golden brown

6. Once the mutton is cooked, remove the pieces from the pressure cooker and shred them using a fork. Keep aside. Retain the mutton stock.

7. When the grains and dals are cooked, open the pressure cooker and add the mutton stock to it. Stir well. After a couple of minutes, add the shredded mutton.

8. Add some water if necessary and cook on low heat for 3–4 hours, stirring occasionally.

9. In a separate pan, fry the remaining onion until golden-brown and add it to the haleem. To reduce the spice level, add lime juice. The consistency of the dal should be semi-thick and not pasty. This is how I like it.

10. Garnish with mint leaves, fried onions and chopped coriander and serve with tandoori roti.

SHILPA'S SECRET: Haleem can be frozen in an airtight container for up to three weeks. Vegetarians can replace mutton with jackfruit as both have the same texture.

Dal Diva ❧

Imli ki dal is a rustic Konkan dish that the royals of Maharashtra enjoyed. It has the perfect amount of tanginess and sweetness and is a break from the usual dal we all have regularly. I call it Dal Diva because I find everyday dal very boring and this is my way of glamming it up.

Serves: 4
Nutritional value:
528 kcal (Carbs: 65 g,
Protein: 49 g, Fats: 8 g)

1 tbsp ghee
1 tsp mustard seeds
8–10 curry leaves
¼ tsp asafoetida
1 tbsp tamarind, soaked
Salt, to taste
1 tsp turmeric powder
1 tsp red chilli powder
1 tsp fenugreek seeds powder
1 cup split pigeon peas, boiled and mashed
Fresh or dry coconut to garnish
½ a bunch of fresh coriander

1. Add ghee in a pan on medium heat. Once it's hot, add the mustard seeds, curry leaves and asafoetida. Mix for a minute.

2. Add salt, turmeric, chilli and fenugreek powders.

3. Squeeze pulp from the tamarind and add to the mashed dal. Mix well.

4. Garnish with coconut and coriander and serve with steamed rice.

Mint and Lemon Juice

Green Juice

ABCG Red Juice

Pumpkin Soup

Chickpea and Sweet Potato Chaat

Poached Eggs and Chickpeas

All-Natural Nutrition Bar

Pumpkin, Peanut Butter and Oat Bars

Bhindi Kurkure

Tauthe Curry

Mom's Bangude Bake (Mackerel Bake)

Shilpa's Treasure Pulao

Jodhpuri Mutton Cooked Rajwada-Style

Three-Layer Pasta (Stage 1)

Three-Layer Pasta (Stage 2)

Three-Layer Pasta (Stage 3)

Three-Layer Pasta (Stage 4)

Three-Layer Pasta (Ready to bake)

Three-Layer Pasta

Biringe Biryani

Man-Thai Green Curry

Fruit and Nut Chia Salad

Cammy's Coconut Cake

Yogi Bowl 1

Yogi Bowl 2

Party Presentation 1

Party Presentation 2

Party Presentation 3

Baking a cake with Viaan on his fifth birthday

Viaan's birthday cake

Roasted turkey on Christmas

Preparing Christmas dinner with Raj

Gluten-Free Pasta in Veggie Pesto Sauce ✍

My son loves his veggies, but a lot of kids don't like them at all. That's why I've included this recipe in my book. It's a way for children to eat the vegetables they need. I've made this dish for my son's play dates and his friends love it. Their mums have even called me later, surprised that their child ate vegetables. So mission accomplished.

Serves: 2
Nutritional value:
318 kcal (Carbs: 36 g,
Protein: 3 g, Fats: 18 g)

4 heads broccoli, cooked or steamed
½ cup spinach
2 tbsp olive oil
3 tbsp cream or whole milk
2 tbsp pine nuts
½ tsp Italian seasoning
Salt and black pepper powder, to taste
4–5 basil leaves
3 garlic cloves, chopped, plus ½ tsp grated garlic
½ onion, sliced thinly (optional)
1 cup cooked pasta (gluten-free)

1. Put some water to boil. Take the spinach in a large colander. Pour boiling water in the colander until the spinach is completely wilted. Then cool under cold water and press the spinach into a ball, squeezing out all the water. Roughly chop the spinach. Puree it in a blender with the broccoli.

2. Transfer the pureed spinach and broccoli into a bowl. Add the grated garlic, 1 tsp olive oil, cream, pine nuts, Italian seasoning, salt, pepper and basil leaves. Mix it all together in a blender and set aside.

3. In a pan, heat the remaining olive oil and sauté the chopped garlic for a minute. Add the onions and fry for a couple of minutes. Add the pasta and spinach puree into the pan and mix well. Check for seasoning and serve hot.

SHILPA'S TIP: You can add half a cup of chicken or paneer to this pasta. Add half a green chilli if you like it spicy.

Mom's Bangude Bake (Mackerel Bake)

This is my mother's signature recipe. She usually made it on Sundays, with a full mackerel, and we'd have it either with dosa or tamatar ka saar. It has the perfect mix of tangy, sweet and spicy flavours. This dish in the book is an ode to my mother.

Serves: 6–8 people
Nutritional value:
200 kcal (Carbs: 5 g,
Protein: 0 g, Fats: 20 g)

4 tsp coconut oil
25 dry red chillies, plus
8–10 fresh green chillies,
chopped
2 tbsp coriander seeds
1 tsp cumin seeds
1 tsp fenugreek seeds
2 tsp black peppercorns
2 tsp turmeric powder
6–8 flakes garlic
A ball of tamarind, the
size of 3 limes
Salt, to taste
1 pinch asafoetida
2-inch piece ginger,
chopped
1 full pod garlic, crushed
12 mackerels
½ cup coriander leaves,
chopped

1. In a pan, heat 2 tsp coconut oil and fry the red chillies, coriander seeds, cumin seeds, fenugreek seeds and peppercorns.

2. Then grind the fried mixture with turmeric powder, garlic flakes, tamarind and salt into a fine paste, adding very little water. Add the asafoetida and set aside.

3. Mix the chopped green chillies, ginger, garlic with the remaining coconut oil. Add this mixture to the paste.

4. Clean the mackerels and make 2–3 horizontal slits in each. Coat them with the masala and keep them in a flat, greased vessel and bake until it dries. Garnish with chopped coriander.

SHILPA'S TIP: Although this recipe is traditionally made with mackerel, which is my favourite, you can use pomfret or basa as well.

Prawn Curry

This is a tangy dish that I love. I've even served it as a starter in a canapé. To make it more interesting, I've also served it with pani puri. Prawn on crisp toast is another favourite. Just toast the bread slice, slather on some butter, cut in into six pieces and place the prawn on each piece and serve.

Serves: 2
Nutritional value:
777 kcal (Carbs: 41 g,
Protein: 106 g, Fats: 21 g)

½ kg medium prawns,
shelled and deveined
1 egg
1 pinch black pepper
powder
Juice of 1½ lemons
2 tbsp vegetable oil
1 tsp cumin seeds
3 onions, chopped
1 tbsp ginger–garlic paste
3 tomatoes, chopped
½ tsp garam masala
½ tsp coriander powder
½ tsp turmeric powder

1. Mix the egg, black pepper and lemon juice in a bowl and marinate the prawns in this for a couple of hours.

2. In a wok, heat the oil and add the cumin seeds. When they start sputtering, add the chopped onions and cook till they turn golden–brown.

3. Now add the ginger–garlic paste and, after a couple of minutes, add the tomatoes and let them cook. Do not let the water dry out completely.

4. Then add the garam masala, coriander and turmeric powders, chicken masala and 1 tablespoon of water. Let the masalas soak for 2 minutes and add salt. Finally, add the red and green chillies.

5. In a frying pan, add the butter and the marinated prawns. After a minute, add the masala mixture. Cover the pan and cook for 5 minutes. Garnish with chopped coriander and serve hot.

½ tsp store-bought
chicken masala
½ tsp salt
3 whole red chillies
2 green chillies
1 tsp butter
A few sprigs chopped
coriander

SHILPA'S SECRET: All sea food at my home is marinated in lemon, salt and turmeric. It takes away the fishy odour. Also, don't overcook the prawns; they become rubbery. Prawns take just 3–5 minutes to cook. The minute the prawns curl and turn opaque, you know they're cooked. You should be able to bite into the prawn and not fight with it. Add the prawns in the masala just before you are ready to serve. Use the leftover masala to make a prawn sandwich or prawn biryani.

Kori Roti 🌿

Kori roti is a popular spicy Mangalorean dish. It is a combination of chicken curry and crisp dry wafers made from boiled rice. The wafers are basically sun-dried dosas that can be broken like a papad. This is my favourite comfort food. Whenever it's served, you know it's a celebration. Whether it was a naming ceremony or we were visiting a relative's house, I always looked forward to having kori roti.

Serves: 2
Nutritional value:
1782 kcal (Carbs: 266 g,
Protein: 103 g, Fats: 34gg)

50 g tamarind
200 g jaggery
2 tbsp vegetable oil
¼ tsp brown mustard seeds
A few curry leaves
¼ tsp fenugreek powder
¼ tsp asafoetida
3 medium onions, chopped
1 tsp ginger–garlic paste
2 tomatoes, chopped
1 tsp cumin powder

1. Soak the tamarind and jaggery in water and extract the pulp. Set aside.

2. In a wok, heat the oil. Add the mustard seeds, curry leaves, fenugreek powder and asafoetida. After 30 seconds, add the onions and fry them till they turn brown. Add ginger–garlic paste and tomatoes.

3. Once the mixture is cooked, add the dry powders, green chillies and pulp of tamarind and jaggery. Continue to stir till the masala turns brown.

4. Add the chicken pieces and salt, and mix well. Let the chicken cook over low heat, stirring occasionally, till it is tender.

5. When the chicken is cooked, add the coconut milk and let it simmer for a few minutes just before serving.

½ tsp garam masala
½ tsp chicken masala
½ tsp turmeric powder
½ tsp red chilli powder
½ tsp coriander powder
10 green chillies, finely chopped
½ kg chicken (boneless or with bone)
Salt, to taste
Milk of 2 large coconuts

SHILPA'S SECRET: My mum used skimmed milk instead of coconut milk to make kori roti to bring down the calories. But if you're using milk, make sure you turn off the heat right before it boils, else the milk will curdle.

Although boneless chicken is fine, I prefer using chicken on the bone as it brings out the flavour in the dish.

You can buy the 'roti' from Mangalore stores or have the chicken curry with dosas or appams.

Shilpa's Treasure Pulao ✿ ▶

This is a simple pulao recipe that I whip up when I am struggling to decide what to cook. It pairs well with cucumber raita, dal, chicken or any other curry. It's a permanent fixture at all occasions—parties or pujas—at my house and is always appreciated by guests.

Serves: 3
Nutritional value:
768 kcal (Carbs: 53 g,
Protein: 4 g, Fats: 60 g)

3 tbsp vegetable oil
1 big onion, julienned
1 bay leaf
3 star anise
2 black cardamoms
5 cloves
1 tsp coriander powder
1 tsp cumin powder
1 tbsp garam masala
Juice of ½ lemon
1 tsp salt

1. Heat the vegetable oil in a wok on medium heat and fry the onions till they are golden brown. Next, add the bay leaf, star anise, black cardamoms and cloves. Mix well.

2. Add the powdered spices and mix for a couple of minutes till they are fragrant.

3. Add the corn, making sure it is partly cooked before you add the rice. You can also steam it separately if you want to save time.

4. Mix in the ghee and the rice, along with water, vegetable stock and lemon juice. Cook for 15 minutes in a pressure cooker. If you want to cook it without pressure, then add 1¾ cup water. Season well and serve hot after removing the whole spices.

½ tsp cayenne pepper
½ tsp black pepper powder
½ cup fresh corn
1 tbsp ghee
1 cup basmati rice,
washed and soaked for 15
minutes
2 cups water
1 veg or chicken stock
cube, soaked in 4 tbsp
warm water

VARIATION: Check if the vegetable cubes are low in salt. Normally, stock cubes are pre-salted, so I hunt for the low-sodium ones. You can substitute corn with green peas or chicken. Nonvegetarians can substitute the vegetable stock cubes with chicken stock cubes.

Jodhpuri Mutton Cooked Rajwada-Style ✿

I first came to know about this dish from a documentary I was watching a few years ago. Warriors in Rajasthan would make this mutton dish while in the midst of battle. They could only carry foods that would keep for months with them. So while dry masalas and onions could be taken, perishable items like tomatoes and lemons couldn't. So they came up with this dish which has very few ingredients. This just goes to show that you don't require too many ingredients to cook a tasty meal.

Serves: 2
Nutritional value:
906 kcal (Carbs: 1 g,
Protein: 203 g, Fats: 10 g)

½ kg boneless mutton and
½ kg mutton with bone,
sliced thinly
Salt, to marinate the
mutton
2 tbsp coriander powder
3 tbsp red chilli powder
2 tbsp raw mango
powder
2 tbsp garlic paste
1 tsp red chilli pickle or
mango pickle
5 tbsp plain yoghurt
2 tsp mustard oil

1. Marinate the mutton for a couple of hours with all the ingredients except the mustard oil so that the mutton expels the water.

2. Heat the mustard oil in a wok and add the marinated mutton pieces. Cook for 30 minutes over low heat, and cover.

3. After 20 minutes, remove the cover and place a roti on top of it. Place a piece of burning coal on it. Pour 1 tsp of ghee, for a smoky flavour, and cover it with a lid.

4. Serve the mutton with the smoky roti.

SHILPA'S TIP: Vegetarians can replace mutton with colocasia root or jackfruit. This dish can also be made with chicken instead of mutton.

Three-Layer Pasta 🌱

This is a one-stop dish. Every home should have a one-dish wonder that they put on the table when guests come over, and this is mine. My cook and I came up with this recipe. It is our take on the shepherd's pie that's served in England. We added pasta, and this amalgam of English meets Italian meets Indian is a cracking combination. While some people prefer pasta in red sauce, others like it in white sauce. This recipe, however, makes use of both. This is a hearty, wholesome, high-fibre, high-protein dish. It has three layers topped with Cheddar or mozzarella cheese (if you are not lactose-intolerant). When layered in a glass casserole, it looks very appealing and colourful. I swear by this dish and it is a permanent fixture at all my parties or on days when I want a fuss-free meal that is comforting. The prep looks long-drawn-out, but trust me, this 'one' dish is worth it all.

Serves: 6
Nutritional value:
2455 kcal
(Carbs: 273 g, Protein: 104 g, Fats: 105 g)
Soya keema masala: 974 kcal (Carbs: 66 g, Protein: 65 g, Fats: 50 g)
Pasta: 988 kcal (Carbs: 165 g, Protein: 37 g, Fats: 20 g)
Tomato sauce: 141 kcal (Carbs: 24 g, Protein: 0 g, Fats: 5 g)
Potato white sauce: 352 kcal (Carbs: 18.5 g, Protein: 2 g, Fats: 30 g)

For the soya keema masala:
2 tbsp oil

1. To make the keema, heat oil in a pressure cooker and add the cumin powder and onions and cook them till they become brown. Then add the ginger–garlic paste and green chilli and mix well for a few minutes.

2. Next, add the chopped tomatoes and the remaining powder masalas and let it roast for two minutes.

3. Add the ready-made soya keema and peas and let the keema cook for three whistles.

4. Boil the pasta in water. After 7–8 minutes, check if it's done. It should be al dente, not overcooked. Strain and set aside. Make sure you pour cold water over the cooked pasta as soon as it's done so that it doesn't clump together.

5. In a frying pan, heat olive oil and add the garlic and mushrooms and cook well. Once the mushrooms are done (the size has almost halved), add the vegetables along with the spinach.

2 onions, chopped
1 tsp ginger–garlic paste
1 green chilli, finely
chopped
2 tomatoes, chopped
1 tsp coriander powder
1 tsp cumin powder
½ tsp garam masala
½ tsp turmeric powder
Salt, to taste
½ tsp chicken masala (or
veg cube for vegetarians)
200 g soya keema
100 g shelled green peas

For the pasta
200 g penne or fusilli
3 tsp olive oil
5 cloves garlic, finely
chopped
200 g mushrooms, each
sliced into 3 pieces
100 g French beans,
chopped
100 g carrots, chopped
2 bunches of spinach,
chopped finely
A few basil leaves
A pinch of sugar
1 tsp milk or almond milk
or fresh cream
Black pepper powder, to
taste
Salt and oregano, to taste

6. Add the basil leaves, salt, pepper and milk or fresh cream and mix well.

7. Once the veggies are properly done—they should have a bite—season with black pepper powder, salt and oregano. Let the pasta and vegetables cook for 5 minutes with the lid on. Set aside.

8. To make the tomato sauce heat 1 cup of water in a pressure cooker, but don't bring it to a boil. Add the tomatoes along with the garlic, onion and chilli powder. Season with salt and cook for two whistles.

9. When it has cooled down, transfer the contents into a mixer and blend.

10. Remove from the mixer and pass it through a sieve.

11. Once it's strained, add the paste to a heated frying pan along with butter, salt, pepper and oregano. Mix well for 3–4 minutes till the sauce is ready.

12. To make the white sauce mix the butter and flour in a frying pan over medium heat. Brown the flour slightly for 3–4 minutes and then add the warm milk, pepper and salt and keep stirring for 5 minutes till all the lumps are dissolved and it thickens. If the consistency is too thick, add some more milk to thin it. Add the mashed potatoes and set aside.

13. To assemble the pasta, grease a baking dish with butter.

14. Spread the pasta with vegetables.

15. Spread the tomato sauce over the pasta.

16. Add the soya keema.

17. Add the potato white sauce.

2 tbsp Parmesan or Cheddar cheese
2 tbsp bread crumbs

For the tomato sauce:
1 cup of water
5 tomatoes, chopped (boiled for 5 minutes and skin peeled)
2–3 garlic cloves, finely chopped
½ onion, chopped
1 tsp Kashmiri chilli powder
Salt, to taste
1 tsp butter
Salt, black pepper powder and oregano, to taste

For the potato white sauce:
2 tbsp butter
2 tbsp flour
1 cup milk or almond milk, warmed
¼ tsp black pepper powder
½ tsp salt
1½ cup mashed potatoes

18. Sprinkle grated Parmesan or Cheddar cheese with the bread crumbs.
19. Bake it in the oven at 190°C for 12–15 minutes. Serve hot.

SHILPA'S SECRET: Assemble this in a glass casserole so your guests can see the three coloured layers. Sometimes, I add sweet potatoes to the regular ones to mix it up. In that case, make sure the soya keema is a bit spicier. Prepare the potato white sauce just before you intend to use it, otherwise, it tends to thicken a lot more as it stands.

Biringe Biryani

This is a Persian biryani. There is always a debate about which biryani is better: the Hyderabadi, Lucknowi, Delhi or Kolkata. I'm not going to tell you which one's the best. But since you've tried all of these, why not give this biryani a shot, especially since it originated in Persia? I first had this Persian biryani when I went to Karachi and I loved it so much that I was determined to bring this dish back to India. The chef at my hotel was generous enough to share his recipe and every time I've cooked this biryani, my guests have loved it.

Serves: 6
Nutritional value:
1202 kcal (Carbs: 68 g,
Protein: 210 g, Fats: 10 g)

1 cup rice
2 tbsp ghee
1 big onion, sliced long
½ tsp cumin seeds
1–2 black cardamoms
3 green cardamoms
1 tsp fenugreek seeds
5 cloves
2 bay leaves
2 cinnamon sticks
1 tsp Kashmiri chilli powder
1 tsp black pepper powder
1 tsp salt
3 tsp biryani masala

1. Wash the rice three times and soak it for 30 minutes. Add water and cook it in a pressure cooker.

2. While the rice is cooking, in a large wok, heat the ghee and fry the sliced onions till they are golden brown. Now add the spices and 1½ tsp biryani masala.

3. Add the ginger–garlic paste and cook till the oil separates.

4. Now add the chicken and fry the mixture for at least 10 minutes. Cover the wok with a net or perforated lid.

5. Add the tomato paste to the wok and mix well. Let it cook for 5 minutes. Then add the yoghurt and cook for 8–10 minutes. Check the chicken, as it tends to stick to the base when mixed with yoghurt. Now add the remaining biryani masala.

5 tsp ginger–garlic paste
1 kg chicken
1 cup tomato paste
½ cup yoghurt
1-inch ginger, julienned
3 green chillies, julienned
1 tbsp lemon juice
Juice from grated beets
1 tbsp kewra water

6. When the rice is cooked, strain it and drain the water completely.

7. To assemble the biryani, take a deep pan, and layer half the rice at the bottom. Now layer the chicken on top of the rice, and scatter the julienned ginger and green chilli and add the lemon juice, making sure it covers most of the chicken. Add the remaining rice and with your hand sprinkle some water that's left behind when you boil a beetroot. This will ensure some of the rice takes on a lovely red hue. Finally, add the kewra water. Make holes in the biryani so that the air trapped in the layers can escape.

8. Cook the biryani over low heat for 20 minutes. Serve hot.

Baked Courgette with Fresh Veggies 🌱 ▶

This works wonderfully as a side dish. It's one of my popular dishes and I've often had requests to serve it.

Serves: 2
Nutritional value:
280 kcal (Carbs. 49 g,
Protein: 3 g, Fats: 8 g)

1 tsp mustard oil
1 onion, chopped
1 radish, chopped
1 capsicum, chopped
1 potato, chopped
1 beetroot, chopped
½ tsp cumin seeds
Salt and black pepper
powder, to taste
½ tsp oil
2 courgettes
A few sprigs coriander,
chopped

1. Heat oil in a wok over medium heat. Add the onion, radish, capsicum, potatoes and beetroot and stir-fry them. Add the cumin seeds and season with salt and pepper. Set aside.

2. Slice the courgettes in half, lengthwise, and deseed them. In a non-stick pan, heat ½ tsp oil and cook the courgette on both sides for 7 minutes each. Cook it cut-side down first.

3. Fill the courgette halves with the vegetable mix and bake at 180°C for 20 minutes. Garnish with chopped coriander and serve hot.

SHILPA'S SECRET: If you don't want to use the vegetables mentioned here, you can replace them with any others that you prefer. That's the beauty of this dish. I've used bottle gourd instead of potato sometimes and it tastes just as good. I've chosen these particular ingredients because they go well with each other.

VARIATION: You can also sprinkle some goat's cheese or Cheddar cheese on top before baking.

SHILPA'S MANTRA

If you're a lover of cold coffee, blend 10 tsp decaf coffee (especially for kids), 6 tsp Agave syrup or 10 tsp jaggery with ¾ cup water and sugar. Pour this into an ice cube tray and freeze. Whenever you want to have cold coffee, take a couple of cubes in a glass, add milk and your coffee is ready.

You can also make a concentrate of lemon juice similarly. Blend the juice of 6 lemons, ½ cup mint leaves, 5 tsp honey, 1 tsp rock salt, 2 tsp jaggery powder, 1 tsp dry mango powder, ½ tsp salt with a ¾ glass of water. And when you're thirsty or guests come over, add some more water to this and it's ready to serve.

Man-Thai Green Curry 🌿 ⏵

This curry is an original. While coconut is a common ingredient in both Thai and Mangalorean cuisines, other items like galangal, lemongrass and bird's eye chillies are not easily found in Indian pantries. Keeping that in mind I decided to give the Thai Green Curry a Mangalorean twist and came up with 'Man-Thai Green Curry'. Simple, everyday ingredients like dried chillies, mustard seeds, curry leaves and Indian ginger bring this dish alive with a burst of flavours. We all enjoy this one and I am sure you will too.

Serves 1
Nutritional Value:
1852 kcal
(Carbs: 54 g, Proteins: 112 g, Fats: 132 g)

2 tbsp coconut oil or sesame oil or vegetable oil
½ tsp mustard seeds
7–8 curry leaves
3 dry red chillies
1½ tbsp ginger
2½ tbsp green Thai curry paste
1 bowl coconut milk (thin)
1½ tsp rice flour
1 bowl pre-steamed broccoli
½ bowl parboiled or steamed sweet potato or pumpkin
3–4 lime leaves
1 tsp salt
1 bowl coconut milk (thick)
1 tsp jaggery or sugar
Freshly chopped coriander leaves

1. Heat the oil over a medium flame and add the mustard seeds, curry leaves, dry red chillies and ginger and mix well. Now add the green Thai curry paste. Add a little bit of water (so the paste does not stick to the pan) and stir.

2. Take ½ bowl of thin coconut milk and add the rice flour to it. Use a whisk to blend it in and take out any lumps. Now add the remaining ½ bowl of thin coconut milk and mix well.

3. Now add the rice flour–coconut milk mixture to the pan, along with the steamed vegetables. Add a little amount of water, put a lid and cook over low heat for 8–10 minutes. Add the lime leaves and salt to taste.

4. Mix in the thick coconut milk and cook for 2 minutes over low heat. Add the jaggery or sugar.

5. Garnish with fresh coriander leaves and serve it with piping hot rice (laced with ghee).

SHILPA'S TIP: If you want to make this nonvegetarian, add 500 g boneless chicken, cut into small pieces and stir-fried for 4–5 minutes.

Desserts

Chhena Sandesh 🌱

My son loves pedas, so I've come up with this recipe to give him what he wants without buying it from a sweet shop.

Makes: 10–12 pieces
Nutritional value:
600 kcal (Carbs: 47 g,
Protein: 31 g, Fats: 32 g)

1 litre full-fat milk + 1
tsp milk
1 tbsp lemon juice
4 tbsp Stevia sugar
¼ tsp kewra essence
5 saffron threads
A few toasted pistachios

1. Boil the milk on high heat. Add the lemon juice and keep stirring till the milk curdles. Let the whey separate from the chhena, then put it in a strainer lined with a muslin cloth. Pour water and rinse the chhena in the cloth to remove the smell of lemon.

2. Squeeze out the excess water. Knead the chhena on a thick wooden surface like you would with dough, to make it smooth. Once all the moisture has dried up, add the sugar and kewra essence.

3. Put the chhena in a pan over low heat.

4. Combine the saffron with 1 tsp milk and add to the pan. Heat the chhena until all the moisture evaporates.

5. Remove, cool and make flat discs. Garnish with toasted pistachios.

Rice Pudding—Manni ✧

This is the south Indian version of phirni—and one of my favourite comfort foods. Also, because it has jaggery and not sugar, I don't even need to wait until my usual Sunday binge to eat it when I'm craving something sweet.

Serves: 8–10
Nutritional value:
750 kcal (Carbs: 98 g,
Protein: 6 g, Fats: 37 g)

1 cup rice
1 cup freshly scraped
coconut
1½ cups scraped jaggery
4 cardamoms
Salt, to taste
2 tsp ghee

1. Rinse the rice and soak it in water for 30 minutes.

2. Grind the rice along with the coconut and make it into a fine paste. Transfer the paste into a wok, add 6 cups of water and mix well. Add the jaggery, cardamoms, salt and ghee.

3. Place the wok with the mixture on low heat and keep stirring for 1 hour or till it thickens and becomes paste-like.

4. Pour the mixture on to a greased plate and allow it to cool completely. Cut into diamond-shaped pieces and serve.

SHILPA'S TIP: This can be stored in the refrigerator for 3–4 days.

Moong Dal or Chana Dal with Sago Payasam 🌱 ▶

This is one of the first desserts I made on my YouTube channel. I always think of my grandmother while making it. Her payasam was delicious; I hope mine is as good as hers.

Serves: 6–8
Nutritional value:
3620 kcal (Carbs: 663 g,
Protein: 62 g, Fats: 80 g)

100 g sago
1 cup of either split green gram or split Bengal gram
Milk of 1 coconut, thick and thin
Salt, to taste
½ kg scraped jaggery
1 tsp crushed cardamom
10–15 pieces each of cashew nuts and raisins
2 tbsp ghee

1. Soak the sago in water for 2–3 hours. Drain the water and keep the sago aside for half an hour.

2. Cook the dal in a pressure cooker for one whistle and place in a big dish. To the pressure cooker, add the remaining dal water, dal and sago and cook over medium heat.

3. Extract the milk of a coconut in a mixer by adding half a glass of water. Strain the milk and set aside. Put the coconut back in the mixer with enough water and grind again for 2 minutes. Strain this water.

4. When the dal and sago mixture is boiling, add the second, thin milk along with a little salt. Keep stirring because the sago tends to stick to the bottom.

5. As you are stirring, keep on adding pieces of jaggery, till you get the desired sweetness. Now add the powdered cardamom and raisins and cashews. Keep stirring.

6. Finally, add the thick coconut milk and ghee. Take off the heat and serve hot.

Two-Minute Pudding ✌

Easy, quick and delicious! With no compromise on taste and good calories.

Serves: 2
Nutritional value:
763 kcal (Carbs: 57 g,
Protein: 10 g, Fats: 55 g)

2 tbsp crunchy almond
butter or peanut butter
1 banana, peeled and
sliced
4 digestive biscuits,
crushed
3 tsp vegetable oil
A pinch of cinnamon
powder
½ cup melted dark
chocolate

1. Combine the biscuits with the vegetable oil to form a rough crumble.

2. Layer the crumble at the bottom of two shot glasses. Top it with banana slices, almond butter and finally melted dark chocolate. Sprinkle the cinnamon powder on top. Serve.

Fruit and Nut Chia Salad ▶

I could live on this salad! Simple, quick and healthy—that's the key word. When I can't wait for my Sunday binge and find myself craving sweets (I have those days too, honestly), this becomes my go-to dessert. It can be had for breakfast, as a dessert for kids in a mason jar, or put in shot glasses as a party dessert. You will love me for this one!

Serves: 4
Nutritional Value: 795 kcal (Carbs: 39 g, Proteins: 9 g, Fats: 67 g)

For the nut brittle:
2 tbsp jaggery sugar
8–10 chopped almonds
8–10 chopped pistachios
4 tbsp water

For the chia seed mixture:
1½ cups chilled coconut milk (thick)
3 tbsp chia seeds
3 tbsp maple syrup (more if you like it sweeter)
½ tsp vanilla essence
¼ tsp cinnamon powder

Fruits:
Papaya
Kiwi
Fresh figs or soaked dry-fruit
Banana
Pomegranate
Or whatever fruit is in season

1. To make the nut brittle, mix the sugar and water in a non-stick pan over medium heat to caramelize the sugar. Add the nuts and stir until combined. Spread the mixture on a silicon mat or lightly greased plate to cool.

2. For the chia seed mixture, combine all the ingredients in a bowl and keep the mixture in the fridge overnight.

3. To serve, layer the fruits and the chia seed mixture alternately. Top with pomegranate and nut brittle. Serve cold.

Two-Minute Ice Cream ❧

Who says you can't enjoy ice cream without feeling guilty?

Serves: 1
Nutritional value:
452 kcal (Carbs: 33 g,
Protein: 8 g, Fats: 16 g)

1 banana, frozen overnight
4 tbsp almond butter
1 tbsp honey
¼ tsp or a pinch of cinnamon

1. Combine all the ingredients in a blender and serve chilled.

Coconut Rava Laddoo 🌿

I love this recipe because the laddoos can be made fresh and easily at home. They are also gluten- and lactose-free. Since kids love getting their hands dirty, it's a fun activity to bond with your child. My son and I make these all the time and he shows them off to his friends. They're perfect to serve at parties, in kids' tiffins and even for pujas as prasad.

Makes: 10
Nutritional value:
1061 kcal (Carbs: 72 g,
Protein: 11 g, Fats: 81 g)

¼ cup ghee
10 cashews, broken into halves
4 tsp raisins
½ tsp cardamom powder
1 cup semolina, roasted and ground in a mixer
¾ cup demerara sugar or coconut sugar
½ cup desiccated coconut, roasted
½ cup almond milk or water

1. In a pan over low heat, use 1 tbsp of ghee to roast the cashews and raisins, and then add cardamom powder.

2. Add the semolina and the sugar and mix well.

3. Now add half of the roasted desiccated coconut and almond milk or water and stir. After a couple of minutes, take the mixture off the gas and transfer to a plate to cool.

4. After 7–8 minutes, grease your hands with a spoonful of ghee and spread the remaining coconut on one side of the plate. Gently make small, round laddoos of the mixture and roll them in the desiccated coconut. Serve them hot or cold.

SHILPA'S SECRET: The laddoos last 3–4 days and even longer if you store them in the refrigerator and if the coconut is dry and roasted.

Bread and Butter Pudding ✿

While I've included this in the dessert section, it is actually a breakfast dish—a glorified version of French toast. The only difference is that the bread is crispy, so you get a crunch. I've seen my mum make this often and have modified it.

Serves: 4
Nutritional value:
1601 kcal (Carbs: 184 g,
Protein: 70 g, Fats: 65 g)

8–10 slices of wholewheat
bread
5 tbsp melted butter
2 cups whole milk
8 tsp brown sugar or
5 tbsp agave syrup
½ tsp cinnamon powder
4 eggs
2 tsp vanilla extract
A pinch of salt

1. Beat the milk, sugar, cinnamon powder, eggs, vanilla extract, salt and 1 tsp butter well.

2. Apply butter on both sides of the bread slices and stack them one on top of the other. Then cut the bread into quarters.

3. In a 6x4″ glass casserole, put a layer of bread pieces and pour some of the egg mixture over it. Sprinkle raisins on top of this layer. Now place the second layer and pour the remaining wet mixture.

4. Bake for 40–45 minutes at 180°C. Serve with vanilla sauce or chocolate ganache.

SHILPA'S SECRET: Use a loaf of bread from the bakery instead of the sliced bread available in grocery stores. You can also add some rum! If you're serving this at a party, pour rum on top and flambé it. It'll be a sight to behold.

Pratibha Aunty's Crazy Cake ❧

Pratibha Aunty is my paternal aunt and this is her recipe. I was ten years old when I took my first ever flight—alone—to Bangalore where Pratibha Aunty lives. I still remember running down from my cousin's room to the kitchen because of the smell of baking cake. She loves to cook and baked practically every day. There was never a cakeless day in her house and the credit for my love for baking goes entirely to her. Make this one quick to become a hero. You'd be crazy NOT to make it!

Makes 1 6-inch cake
Nutritional value:
445 kcal (Carbs: 55 g,
Protein: 0 g, Fats: 25 g)

1½ cups sifted flour
1 tsp baking soda
½ tsp salt
1 cup sugar
3 tbsp cocoa powder
5 tbsp cooking oil
1 tbsp white vinegar
1 tsp vanilla extract
1 cup cold water

1. Preheat the oven to 350°C. Grease one 6x6" cake pan.

2. Sift the flour, baking soda, salt, sugar and cocoa powder directly into the cake pan. Make three grooves in the dry mixture. Pour oil into one, vinegar into the other and vanilla into the third. Pour cold water over the entire mixture. Beat until the batter is almost smooth. Bake at 350°C for 30–35 minutes. Dust with confectioners' sugar and serve.

Chikki ✿

It's the one thing that satiates my sweet tooth during the week when I don't have any dessert.

Serves: 4
Nutritional value:
730 kcal (Carbs: 50 g,
Protein: 21 g, Fats: 50 g)

1½ cup jaggery
1¼ cups chia seeds,
roasted coconut, sesame
seeds, crushed peanuts,
kurmura or almonds
A pinch of cardamom
powder

1. Grease the kitchen worktop or a thali and set aside.

2. Heat the jaggery in a heavy-bottomed pan and cook over medium heat until a thick syrup is formed.

3. Mix your preferred ingredient(s) into the jaggery syrup, add the cardamom powder and immediately transfer on to the greased kitchen worktop or thali.

4. Let it cool for 30 seconds. Then roll it out as thinly as possible using a greased rolling pin. Let it cool slightly before cutting into smaller pieces. Store in an airtight container once the chikki is completely cooled.

Healthy Veg Cake

I'm sure your first reaction will be: 'Veg cake! What is that?' Trust me when I say that this turns out beautifully and while guests are initially hesitant about eating it, they end up liking it a lot. A huge health advantage here is that it's made with vegetable oil and not butter. So don't go by its name and give this cake a shot.

Makes 1 9-inch cake
Nutritional value:
1538 kcal (Carbs: 210 g,
Protein: 35 g, Fats: 62 g)

1½ cups vegetable or coconut oil
4 eggs
2 cups brown or demerara sugar
3 cups grated carrots or beetroot or papaya
1 cup chopped walnuts
2 cups sifted gluten-free flour
2 tsp baking powder
1 tsp cinnamon
½ tsp salt

1. Preheat the oven to 350°C.
2. Beat the oil and eggs in a bowl. Gradually beat in the sugar. Once the sugar is combined, add the grated vegetables and nuts.
3. In another bowl, sift the flour, baking powder, cinnamon and salt and add it to the wet mixture. Mix the batter well by hand.
4. Pour the batter into a 9x2" greased and floured cake pan. Bake for 55 minutes.
5. For the icing, beat together the butter and cream cheese using an electric mixer. Add the vanilla. Gradually add the confectioners' sugar as you continue beating for a minute or two. Spread the icing evenly on the cake, cut into pieces and serve.

For the icing:
½ cup butter, at room
temperature
1 cup cream cheese, at
room temperature
1 tsp vanilla essence
2¼ cups confectioners'
sugar

VARIATION: Since diabetics have to avoid excess sugar, they can use the following recipe:

Mix together:
5 tbsp cream cheese
1 tsp vanilla essence
½ tsp lemon rind
5–8 drops Stevia

SHILPA'S MANTRA

Considering that I have a sweet tooth, desserts are an important part of my meal. I love to indulge my cravings and believe that desserts can satiate the mind and the soul. Sunday Binges have now become synonymous with me and I want people to know that it is okay to cheat once in a while. My 'cheat day' is Sunday; it's the one day when I don't say 'no' to anything—from rasgullas, rabri and malpuas to kulfi, jalebi and cake! On weekdays, however, I am disciplined and prefer eating guilt-free desserts with healthy fats. So something like the Fruit and Nut Chia Salad shared in the book is perfect for a mid-week sweet!

Yoghurt Strawberry Popsicles ✿

I used to believe I was the only mother who made this for her child until I realized that it's quite common. The popsicles began as a way of getting my son to eat fruits when he was younger. I would mash apples, kiwis and mangoes and make a popsicle. And now even though he's older and enjoys fruits, I still make these for him once in a while.

Makes: 4
Nutritional value:
120 kcal (Carbs: 138 g,
Protein: 26 g, Fats: 23 g)

4–5 strawberries
1 tsp brown sugar
½ tsp lemon juice
10 tbsp thick Greek or
natural yoghurt
3 tbsp honey
1 tsp vanilla essence

1. Puree the strawberries with the brown sugar and a little lemon juice.
2. Mix the yoghurt with honey and vanilla essence and lemon juice.
3. Layer the popsicle mould with alternating layers of strawberry puree and yoghurt.
4. Close and freeze. Serve chilled.

SHILPA'S SECRET: If you don't want to use yoghurt, mash two fruits, add some lemon juice and jaggery or coconut sugar and freeze it. This is great for kids who are teething.

SHILPA'S TIP: Add lemon juice to preserve the fruit so it doesn't become black.

Banana and Oats Pancake ✎

This is an extremely healthy and filling pancake that can be whipped up in less than 10 minutes. It contains the goodness of bananas and oats and substitutes honey for sugar. If you want your pancakes to rise and be fluffy, use baking powder; I use baking soda instead as the pancakes look better and are thicker.

Makes: 8
Nutritional value:
2860 kcal (Carbs: 390 g,
Protein: 46 g, Fats: 124 g)

1 banana, mashed
1 cup oats, roasted and blended
½ cup buttermilk (1½ cups if you're not using eggs)
2 eggs (optional)
½ tsp salt
2–3 tbsp honey
1 tsp baking powder
2 tbsp butter or vegetable oil
¼ tsp cinnamon
1 tsp vanilla extract

1. Take the mashed banana in a large bowl and add eggs. Now add the buttermilk, honey and vanilla. Combine well.

2. Then mix in the blended oats, baking powder (or soda), cinnamon and salt.

3. Heat the non-stick pan. Grease it with butter. Pour a ladle (¼ cup) of the batter on the pan. Flip when you see bubbles on the circumference and cook the other side for 30–40 seconds.

4. Serve with maple syrup or honey.

SHILPA'S TIP: You can add raisins, cranberries, blueberries or even chocolate chips too.

Cammy's Coconut Cake ❧

My son's nanny, Cammy, has been taking care of him since he was born. Viaan adores her and she's a part of my family now. One Christmas, her son was visiting and since she makes her coconut cake for him every time he's in the country, she asked if she could make one for us too. She made it in my house that first time and I've been a fan ever since. It is basically a large macaroon. The beauty of this cake is that it has no flour in it and so is very healthy. And, I don't have to tell you how much I love coconut in any form.

Makes 1 8-inch cake
Nutritional value:
9450 kcal (Carbs: 1172 g,
Protein: 150 g, Fats: 454 g)

1 cup milk or almond milk
750 g demerara sugar
500 g semolina
12 eggs
500 g desiccated coconut
50 g Amul butter
(optional)
150 g ghee
2 tsp vanilla essence
¼ tsp baking powder

1. Heat the milk in a large pan. After about five minutes, add sugar. Stir it continuously for a few minutes and take it off the gas. Now slowly add in the semolina, stirring all the while.

2. Beat the eggs till they turn fluffy and frothy. Add only the froth to the pan with the milk and semolina.

3. Add the desiccated coconut, butter, ghee, vanilla essence and baking powder. Keep mixing this till it becomes fluffy. Keep it covered overnight or for 4–5 hours.

4. The next day, grease an 8-inch baking dish and place butter paper in it. Pour the batter into the dish and bake it in the oven at 160–180°C for 20–25 minutes.

SHILPA'S TIP: If you're not comfortable using butter, use 4 tbsp oil instead.

Papaya Halwa 🌿

This is a gluten-free halwa, so it's much healthier, especially for those who suffer from irritable bowel syndrome.

Serves: 5
Nutritional value:
345 kcal (Carbs: 31 g,
Protein: 0 g, Fats: 25 g)

1 semi-ripe medium
papaya
4 tbsp ghee
½ tsp cardamom powder
4 tbsp poppy seeds
2 tbsp almond powder
4 tbsp sugar
4–5 pistachios, finely
chopped

1. Soak the papaya in cold water for 10–15 minutes and grate it. Set aside.

2. In a deep wok, heat the ghee and add the poppy seeds.

3. After a couple of minutes, add the grated papaya and cardamom powder. Mix well.

4. Add almond powder to this to bind the halwa. Then add the sugar. Cook for another 10 minutes. Garnish with chopped pistachios and serve.

No-Bake Dessert 🌱

This is for all those people who think I'm quite a Grinch when it comes to sweets. This is my family's 'let-go' dessert. I've served this at a kids' party at my home and it's been a big hit.

Makes: 2 pieces
Nutritional value:
3500 kcal (Carbs: 130 g,
Protein: 30 g, Fats: 350 g)

6 Oreo cookies, crushed
250 g butter, melted
1½ cups white chocolate
bits, melted
200 g white chocolate
cream or white chocolate
with Mascarpone cheese
A few marshmallows

1. Combine four of the crushed cookies with the melted butter and press into a baking tray that has a removable bottom.

2. Add the chocolate bits and white chocolate cream on top with the remaining cookie crumbs.

3. Garnish with marshmallows, cut into cubes and serve.

For the dark chocolate ganache:
600 g dark chocolate, chopped
1 cup thickened cream

1. To make the dark chocolate ganache, take the chocolate and cream in a glass or ceramic microwave-safe bowl. Microwave on medium power (50 per cent) for 2–3 minutes, stirring every 30 seconds with a spoon to get a smooth consistency. Keep at room temperature until it has thickened.

VARIATION: To reduce the calorie content, you can use digestive biscuits and dark chocolate ganache walnuts with caramel or peanut butter. You can also use almond butter because it has no sugar.

Coconut, Avocado and Pistachio Pudding ✿

Thankfully, avocados are now available throughout the year in India. Avocados and pistachios have a similar texture. This is a guilt-free pudding that I've even had as a filling breakfast. Combined with chia seeds, it is a powerhouse of energy. And if I talk any more about the benefits of coconut, I'm sure you'll think I have coconut trees growing in my backyard.

Serves: 4
Nutritional value:
1583 kcal (Carbs: 27 g,
Protein: 20 g, Fats: 155 g)

3 ripe avocados
300 ml coconut milk
3–4 tbsp honey
1 tbsp chia seeds
2 tbsp shredded coconut
3 tbsp shelled, chopped pistachios

1. In a food processor, blend the avocados, coconut milk and honey until smooth.
2. Add the chia seeds and blend one more time to combine.
3. Pour the pudding into ramekins and set in the fridge for at least 50 minutes.
4. Top with coconut and pistachios and serve cold.

SHILPA'S TIP: If you find avocado difficult to procure or expensive to buy, replace it with sweet potato. You'll need to puree it and take out the strings though.

Baked Apple Pancake with Jaggery Sauce ❧

This is one of the healthiest desserts I've made and a great idea when you're craving some sweet pancakes.

Serves: 2
Nutritional value:
2189 kcal (Carbs: 256 g,
Protein: 37 g, Fats: 113 g)

For the batter:
2 eggs (optional)
1 cup rice flour or almond flour
½ cup milk
2 tsp vanilla essence
A pinch of cinnamon powder
1 apple, sliced thinly
A few raisins

1. Preheat the oven to 220°C.
2. Mix all the ingredients till a thick batter is formed.
3. Pour the batter into a baking tray using approximately ¼ cup for each pancake. Bake for 15 minutes.

*For the caramel jaggery
sauce:*
50 g butter
250 g jaggery
*1 cup almond milk or
low-fat milk*

4. Melt the butter and jaggery and add the milk to prepare the sauce.

5. Drizzle the caramel–jaggery sauce over the pancakes while serving.

SHILPA'S SECRET: Adding banana to the mixture will make it thick and you'll enjoy the pancake more.

Coconut Pancakes

This is another ode to my Mangalorean roots. I cannot overstate the good properties of coconut, and like the earlier pancake recipe, this one is very healthy too.

Serves: 5
Nutritional value:
1037 kcal (Carbs: 11 g,
Protein: 66 g, Fats: 81 g)

5 eggs, yolks and whites
separated
200 ml almond milk
1 cup coconut flour or
almond flour
½ tsp cinnamon powder
½ tsp vanilla essence
¼ tsp coconut oil

1. Take all the ingredients, except the egg whites and coconut oil, in a large bowl. Mix well and set aside.

2. Whisk the egg whites until they form soft peaks and fold it into the mixture.

3. Once the pancake batter is ready, heat a non-stick pan over medium heat. Pour the batter into the pan, using approximately ¼ cup for each pancake. Let it cook for 3 minutes on each side and serve.

SHILPA'S SECRET: When I fry, I cut an onion in half. I stick a fork into one half, dip it in the coconut oil and spread it around the pan. This way you don't use a lot of oil while cooking but still get the taste of the coconut oil.

Apricot Pudding ✌

Everyone loves custard and I wanted to include a dessert recipe that's very easy to make. And this is it.

Serves: 2
Nutritional value:
420 kcal (Carbs: 63 g,
Protein: 15 g, Fats: 12 g)

½ cup custard powder
20 apricots soaked
overnight and deseeded
4 whole apricots, soaked
overnight
1 tbsp fresh cream or
vanilla ice cream
3 tbsp maple syrup or
brown sugar
A few pistachios, chopped

1. Follow the instructions to make the custard using the custard powder. Set aside.

2. Process the soaked and deseeded apricots in a blender with 250 ml of the soaking water till it forms a puree.

3. Transfer the puree and the whole apricots to a deep pan and bring to a boil over slow medium heat, for about 20–25 minutes. Then add the maple syrup or brown sugar and stir for 5 minutes.

4. Add the apricot puree over the custard and top with fresh cream or vanilla ice cream.

5. Garnish with chopped pistachios and serve.

SHILPA'S TIP: You can also add fruits like strawberries and mangoes when they're in the season, but this is my version of the famous Hyderabadi dish Khubani ka Meetha.

Orange, Ginger and Cardamom Cake

Ginger and cardamom with orange is such a great combination. If you think about it, it's actually a no-brainer. I've realized how good homemade desserts taste compared to the store-bought stuff. This is one of the desserts I especially love to bake. It's a good tea cake.

Makes 1 8-inch cake
Nutritional value:
3040 kcal (Carbs: 222 g,
Protein: 44 g, Fats: 220 g)

For the cake:
250 g refined self-rising flour
200 g unsalted butter
1 tsp cardamom powder
1 tsp grated ginger
3 eggs
200 ml freshly squeezed orange juice
1 tsp vanilla essence
A few almonds, chopped
7–8 raisins

For orange sugar:
Add zest of 1 orange to 150 g castor or demerara sugar, powdered

1. Beat and whisk the butter, eggs, ginger and vanilla essence together and keep aside.
2. Mix the cardamom powder with the flour and add it in batches to the batter.
3. Preheat the oven to 180°C.
4. Add freshly squeezed orange juice to the batter and mix in the chopped almonds or raisins.
5. Line an 8-inch baking tray with butter paper and pour the batter into it. Bake for 30 minutes. Top with orange sugar and serve.

Gulab Jamun Bake ✿

I invented this recipe a few years ago after guests brought freshly made gulab jamuns when they were visiting. We'd all had our fill after the meal, but there were quite a few still left over. That's when I experimented a bit and came up with this bake.

Serves: 6
Nutritional value:
1406 kcal (Carbs: 136 g,
Protein: 22 g, Fats: 86 g)

8 gulab jamuns
200 ml fresh cream
200 ml condensed milk
Saffron, soaked in milk
4 tbsp custard powder,
blended with ½ cup milk

1. Preheat the oven to at 160°C.
2. Cut the gulab jamuns in half and put them in a heat-proof bowl.
3. Mix the fresh cream, condensed milk, saffron and custard milk and pour it on the gulab jamuns.
4. Place the bowl in a baking tray and pour hot water in the baking tray till it is 1-inch high. Bake for 20 minutes and serve hot.

SHILPA'S TIP: If you don't want to use gulab jamuns, you can make this dish with mawa cake or gajar ka halwa or even motichoor laddoos.

If you don't want to make the custard with condensed milk, you can keep it simple and prepare plain custard. Blend ¼ cup custard powder with 2½ cups (625 ml) of milk and add 2 tablespoons of sugar (or maple syrup or agave syrup) and bring this mixture to a boil.

Gooey Brownie Chocolate Love

Brownies are the first thing I made in a cookery class I attended when I was young. So I have a special love for brownies. Well-made brownies really make you feel like the best cook in the world.

Serves: 4
Nutritional value:
5204 kcal (Carbs: 485 g,
Protein: 33 g, Fats: 348 g)

280 g cooking chocolate
250 g butter
3 eggs, yolks and whites separated
250 g castor sugar
1 tsp vanilla essence
110 g refined flour
5–6 marshmallows
A few rum-soaked raisins or walnuts (optional)

1. Preheat the oven to 180°C.
2. Melt the cooking chocolate and butter in a microwave for 2 minutes. Transfer the mixture to a bowl and add the egg yolks, sugar and vanilla essence. Use a whisk or a beater to combine the mixture.
3. Now mix in the flour, raisins and marshmallows.
4. Beat the egg whites until they form a trail, and gradually fold them into the batter so as not to lose any air.
5. Pour the batter into a baking tray lined with butter paper. Bake for 15–18 minutes.
6. Remove from the oven, cut the brownies and serve them by themselves or with vanilla ice cream.

Spiced Fruits Infused with White Wine or Rum ❧

This recipe is for grown-ups. I don't drink alcohol, but we have several guests who do. And this quick dessert has always been popular with them.

Serves: 2
Nutritional value:
1331 kcal (Carbs: 326 g, Protein: 0 g, Fats: 3 g)

½ tsp butter
3–4 star anise
3–4 cloves
3 mace
200 g apples, chopped
200 g apricots, chopped
200 g peaches, chopped
200 g kiwis, chopped
200 g pineapple, chopped
200 g oranges, chopped
1–2 tbsp white wine or rum (depending on how naughty you want it!)
½ tsp garam masala
½ tsp black pepper powder
1 sponge cake

1. Heat the butter in a pressure cooker, and add the whole spices. Mix well.

2. Put all the fruits in a bowl and add the white wine or rum to it along with the garam masala and black pepper powder and let them steep for some time.

3. Then add the fruits to the cooker, mix well and let it stew for 5–10 minutes.

4. Take the fruits off the heat and puree in a blender or using a hand blender.

5. Pour the spiced fruit puree over the sponge cake and serve with vanilla ice cream.

SHILPA'S TIP: You can use any two out of the peaches, kiwi, pineapple and orange, if you want. Just be sure to increase the quantity of the other fruits to 300 grams each.

Deconstructed Apple Pie ✿

Normally, apple pie served in a bakery is a pastry. But it's difficult to make one at home. So this is a simpler way to get the same taste.

2 apples, diced
1 l lemon water
200 g butter
5 tbsp brown sugar
1 tsp cornflour or wheat flour
1 tbsp honey
½ cup milk
1 sponge cake
A few raisins
A pinch of cinnamon powder

1. Soak the apples in plain lemon water for about 15 minutes so they don't go brown.

2. Melt the butter in a pan over medium heat. Add the brown sugar and mix.

3. Add the apples soaked in lemon water to that. Mix for a couple of minutes and add the flour. Set it aside so it cools down.

3. Add honey to the milk so it becomes sweet and mixes it well. Pour the sweetened milk over the sponge cake and soak it well.

4. Gently spread the apples on top of the cake and garnish with raisins.

5. Serve with whipped cream or vanilla ice cream in shot glasses or chai cups and sprinkle some cinnamon powder on top.

SHILPA'S SECRET: The milk makes the sponge cake soft, so make sure you don't skip that step.

Yogi Bowls

My Special Yogi Bowls

I'm a big believer in the transformative power of yoga. Practising it regularly has made a remarkable difference in my body and mind. An experienced yogi eats food that's clean (easy to digest) at the right time and with thought (not allowing anything and everything to be ingested). I've come up with these special quick meals for nourishment and weight management. Just one 6x6" bowl for lunch or dinner is enough.

Pick and choose any of the ingredients from each of the columns to prepare your bowl and you're on your way to a healthy body. They're very filling and you will notice weight loss in just a week. In fact with the right mix of foods, you will see a change the next morning itself because it reduces bloating caused by water retention.

Vegetables	Protein	Legumes	Seeds	Leaves	Dressing oils
Carrot	Chicken	Red kidney	Pumpkin	Rocket	Flaxseed
Radish (raw)	Fish	beans	Flax	Lettuce	Olive
Avocado	Prawns	Moong beans	Chia	Little gem	Coconut
Tomatoes (raw)	Paneer	Black lentils	Sunflower	lettuce	Chilli
Broccoli	Halloumi	Chickpeas		Mixed salad	
Cauliflower	Tofu	Pearl barley			
Pumpkin	Quinoa				
Bottle gourd	Edamame				
Capsicum (raw)	Eggs (in any				
Cucumber (raw)	form—my				
Baby spinach (raw)	favourites				
Purple cabbage	are boiled or				
Regular cabbage	poached eggs)				
Pak choi					

Your bowl should have at least 4 veggies, 1 protein ingredient, a few seeds and one variety of leaves and ½ tsp of the oil of your choice. You can also substitute oil with buttermilk dressing or all these over hot veg or chicken broth.

If it's a lunch meal or before 5 p.m., try adding a couple of raw veggies like tomatoes, lettuce or bell peppers.

Welcome to the Shetty–Kundra Home Restaurant

A few years ago, out of the blue, I hit upon an idea that has changed my life. And trust me, I'm not exaggerating. A few hours before every meal, my cook would ask me what to make. With three people having different tastes, it was quite frustrating to think of what to cook. For me, preparing the meal has never been the hard part; deciding what to cook is. So I came up with the idea of a menu that would include all our favourite foods, mixed with a few healthy ones that we should have. Ever since I typed it out and got it laminated, I find I have a lot of free time because I'm not agonizing over our next meal. Like in a restaurant, we glance through it and place our orders. I've shared it with you below. It's time to make one for yourself too, with the dishes you make at home and some new ones for variety!

Breakfast and snacks
- Rava Idli
- Rice Idli
- Dosa
- Neer Dosa
- Uttapam
- Dahi Vada
- Upma
- Poha (onion/potato)
- Medu Vada
- Masala Oatmeal
- Dalia

- Vegetable Oatmeal
- Patla Poha Bhajile (Sweet with Coconut Milk)

Salads
- Beet Salad (goat's cheese and walnuts)
- Lettuce Salad (pine nuts, cucumber, boiled sweet potatoes, pumpkin)
- Lettuce Salad (boiled eggs, pickled onions, French beans, olives, mayonnaise, corn)
- Lettuce Salad (lemon honey mustard, asparagus, olives, steamed broccoli, pomegranate)
- Apple, Lettuce, Olive, Grated Beetroot, Honey Mustard Sauce, Lemon Salad
- Potato Salad (egg, mayonnaise, corn, diced pineapple)
- Chickpea Chaat Salad

Starters
- Mushroom Stir-Fry with Garlic
- Butter-Garlic Prawns
- Chicken (garlic, ginger/ bean sauce satay)
- Fish Satay
- Kebabs (chicken and mutton)
- Paneer Grill
- Chicken Tikka
- Chicken Bitki
- Stir-Fry Water Chestnuts
- Spring Rolls
- Chicken Dragon Noodles
- Fish/Chicken Fingers (breaded or vermicelli noodles)
- Patra
- Dry Chicken Dragon
- Basil Fish Satay
- Breaded Chops
- Alu Tuk
- Kand Chips
- Sweet Potato Roast
- Dahi Bhalla

Soups
- Mushroom Soup
- Tomato Soup

- Pumpkin Soup
- Carrot Soup
- Barley Soup
- Vegetable/Chicken Clear Soup
- Paya Soup
- Sweet Corn Soup (vegetable/chicken)
- Beetroot Soup
- Tom Yum Soup (prawns/chicken)
- Lemongrass Soup
- Tom Kha Soup

Mains (Vegetarian)

Rice
- Vegetable Corn Pulao
- Vegetable Biryani
- Jeera Rice
- Pot Rice with Mushroom
- Ghee and Onion Pulao

Dals
- Yellow Dal (tur)
- Yellow Dal (moong)
- Kali Dal
- Konkan's Khatti Dal
- Chhola
- Kala Channa (dry/gravy)
- Sprouted Moong Dal
- Five-Dal Mixture
- Chawli Dal

Vegetable Curries and Dry Preparations
- Doodhi/Mushroom/Paneer Curry
- Mutter Paneer (gravy)
- Paneer/Doodhi Kofta Curry
- Mangalorean Cucumber Curry (Tauthe Curry)
- Punjabi Kadhi (corn/onion/palak pakoras)

- Sindhi Kadhi
- Tomato Saar
- Alu Tuk
- Soya Keema
- Pumpkin and Coconut Sabzi
- Okra Dry/Fry
- Puri Bhaji
- Mix Vegetable Sabzi
- Palak Paneer
- Palak Corn
- Karela Makhani
- Jeera Alu
- Dum Alu Kashmiri
- Palak Alu
- Drumstick Coconut (dry)
- Mangalorean-Style Beans
- Brinjal Potato
- Baingan Bharta
- Tinda
- Turi
- Tendli Coconut (dry)
- Methi Alu
- Methi Mutter Malai
- Vegetable Dhansak
- Zucchini and Tofu Stir-Fry
- Sweet Potato and Pea/Broccoli Curry

Rotis
- Moong Chilla
- Keema/Egg/Paneer/Dal/Gobi/Muli Parathas
- Methi Thepla
- Puri

Mains (Nonvegetarian)

Rice
- Pulao (egg/chicken/prawn)
- Biryani (chicken/mutton/egg/prawn/fish)

Curries and Dry Preparations
- Curry (chicken/mutton/egg/prawn)
- Masala (chicken/mutton/egg/prawn/chap)
- Keema (chicken/mutton with potatoes/peas)
- Mutton/Chicken Dry with Coconut
- Kori Roti

Fish
- Fish Fry
- Green/Red Masala (grilled/shallow-fried tilapia/pomfret/mackerel)
- Basa/Sea Bass (Italian/Chinese style)—spring onions, ginger, green chillies, honey, soya
- Olive Fish
- Lemon-Butter Fish
- Fish Curry
- Goan Fish Curry
- Prawn Sukha

Pasta
- Pasta Veg Bake
- Baked Dish (chicken keema/pasta with potatoes)
- Lasagne
- Tofu Stir-Fried (spring opinion, capsicum, mushroom, chillies)
- Stir-Fried French Beans (peanuts)
- Stir-Fried Broccoli/Mushroom/Asparagus/French Beans
- Pasta in Pesto Sauce

Desserts
- Gulab Jamun Bake
- Bread and Butter Pudding
- Coconut Cake
- Chikki (coconut/til)
- Deconstructed Apple Pie
- Dry Fruit Laddoos
- Moong Dal Payasam

Party Menus

Make Your Own Party Menu

A basic party menu should have at least three starters. With this book, you now have many dishes to choose from. Keep it simple by setting up the cold platters before your guests arrive, so you have time to prepare the hot starters. If you don't have time for hot starters, there's no need to worry. The cold starters will do just fine; just add some low-sodium nachos and salsa and olives and no one will miss anything till dinner.

Basics
- 3 different dry fruits (masala cashew nuts, makhanas and pistachios)
- 1 or 2 dips: Hummus/dal/yogurt dip with crudités
- 2 kinds of cheese (Cheddar and Brie) with grapes and dry or fresh figs

Hot starters
- Aloo Tuk (make them in advance, leaving only the fry once the guests arrive)
- Fish Cutlets
- Chicken Bitkis or Seekh Kebabs
- Grilled Paneer or Lotus Root Potato Cutlet

Mains (Nonvegetarian)
- Beetroot Salad with Goat's Cheese/Asparagus and Orange Salad
- Steamed/Grilled Basa with Soya Honey Chilli /Bangda Masala
- Baked Dish with Keema/Soya or Vegetable Pulao
- Prawn Masala or Ghee Jeera Chicken

- Stir-Fry Veg or Beans Stir-Fry
- Dal (any style)

OR

- Gina's Haleem
- Non-Saag Saag
- Dahi Bhalla
- Aloo Gobi
- Dal (yellow/black)
- Rotis/Hot Buttered Pav
- Veg/Corn Pulao

Mains (Vegetarian)
- Halloumi and Grape Salad or Sprouted Moong/Chickpea and Sweet Potato Salad or any salad of your choice
- Konkan Dal (or any dal of your choice)
- Okra Fry
- Baked Dish with Soya
- Egg/Mushroom and Sweet Potato Curry
- Sweet Corn Pulao
- Pomegranate Raita with Cucumber

OR

- Veg Pulao
- Usha Rani's Baingan Bharta
- Tauthe Curry/Dal
- Zucchini Fritters
- Pasta in Pesto Sauce
- Stir-Fry Beans

Dessert
- *Choose any one*
- Chikki for the health-conscious dessert eaters or Baked Gulab Jamun, Moong Dal Payasam

- Bread and Butter Pudding/Deconstructed Apple Pie

Tea
- Always serve or at least ask if your guests would like tea/coffee at the end.
- Mint/Tulsi/Aniseed/Green Tea with Lemon

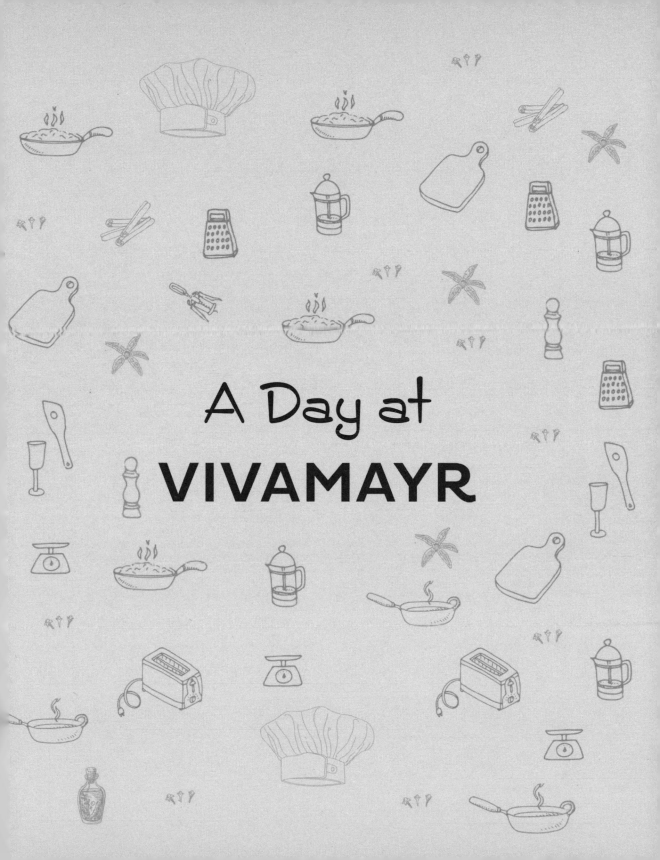

A Day at
VIVAMAYR

Earlier this year, I visited **VIVAMAYR**, a spa in Austria, to unwind and detox—my first holiday since my son was born. On this trip, I enjoyed several healthy recipes, some of which I have shared here (with their permission). All their breads are made using Indian ingredients. It's truly amazing that I had to travel that far to get the best that India has to offer. Their recipes also include spreads. The main aim of these recipes is to alkalize the body. When your body is alkaline and your gut is clean, your health and beauty will be at their best. That is why they have these special spreads as part of their detox plan. They are extremely filling and very simple to prepare. They use curd made from sheep's milk in their recipes, which isn't easily available in India; you can replace it with goat's cheese or almond curd.

Moist Poppy Seed Cake with Warm Raspberry Sauce

Makes 1 9-inch cake
Nutritional value:
4111 kcal (Carbs: 190 g,
Protein: 11 g, Fats: 323 g)

For the cake:
150 g butter
150 g icing sugar, plus
extra for garnishing
6 eggs, whites and yolks
separated
150 g poppy seeds
½ tsp baking powder
80 g ground almonds or
almond flour
A pinch of cinnamon
powder
Grated peel of ½ lemon
½ tsp vanilla sugar
Oil, for the baking pan
100 g slivered almonds

For the raspberry sauce:
400 g raspberries
2 tbsp honey

1. Preheat the oven to 175 °C.

2. In a bowl, beat the butter and half the icing sugar with the egg yolks until it becomes fluffy.

3. Stir in the poppy seeds, baking powder and ground almonds.

4. Now beat the egg whites with the rest of the icing sugar until it forms stiff peaks.

5. Fold the poppy seed mixture and the egg whites alternately into the egg yolk mixture. Stir in the cinnamon powder, grated lemon peel and vanilla sugar.

6. Pour this batter into a greased 9-inch cake or torte pan and bake for 30–40 minutes. After 10 minutes, scatter the slivered almonds over the cake and continue to bake.

7. To make the raspberry sauce, bring ⅓ of the raspberries to a boil with the honey and pass through a strainer. Let it cool slightly and then add the remaining raspberries.

8. Sprinkle the finished cake with icing sugar and serve with raspberry sauce.

Tropical Spread

Serves: 4
Nutritional value:
1458 kcal (Carbs: 35 g,
Protein: 100 g, Fats: 102 g)

500 g goat's cheese
250 g steamed papaya
¼ tbsp mild turmeric
1 tsp grated ginger
½ tbsp linseed oil /olive oil
Rock salt, to taste

1. Place all the ingredients in a food processor or chopper and blend till it obtains a smooth texture.

Avocado Spread: The Calcium Dispenser ꙮ

Serves: 4
Nutritional value:
702 kcal (Carbs: 20 g,
Protein: 16 g, Fats: 62 g)

2 ripe avocados, peeled
and pitted
Juice of ½ lime
200 g cow's milk
(almond milk if you're
lactose intolerant)
1 tsp finely chopped basil
1 tbsp sesame seeds
Rock salt, to taste

1. Combine all the ingredients in a blender until you get a finely processed paste.

Artichoke and Olive Spread: Green Butter ✿

Serves: 4
Nutritional value:
139 kcal (Carbs: 20 g,
Protein: 8 g, Fats: 3 g)

250 g artichoke hearts
10 green olives, pitted
2 tbsp olive oil
3–4 fresh basil leaves
Rock salt, to taste (only
if you're using unsalted
artichoke hearts)

1. Combine all the ingredients in a blender and blend into a creamy paste. Serve with pita bread or crudités.

Almond Spread: Protein Butter ❧

Serves: 4
Nutritional value:
1630 kcal (Carbs: 20 g,
Protein: 50 g, Fats: 150 g)

200 g almonds
1 cup water
Salt, to taste
1 cup walnut oil

1. Put all the ingredients into a blender and mix well.

Beetroot Spread with Potatoes: Red Butter 🌱

Serves: 4
Nutritional Value:
562 kcal
(Carbs: 64 g, Proteins: 8 g,
Fats: 30 g)

300 g cooked floury
potatoes
200 g boiled beetroot
A pinch of ground cumin
Rock salt, to taste
Freshly grated
horseradish, to taste
1 tsp freshly chopped
parsley
2 tbsp olive or hempseed oil

1. Peel the boiled potatoes and press them through a potato ricer.

2. Put the cooked beetroot into a blender and add the potatoes along with the rest of the ingredients. Season with rock salt.

Mediterranean Spread

Serves: 4
Nutritional value:
330 kcal (Carbs: 12 g,
Protein: 12 g, Fats: 26 g)

150 g zucchini, chopped
50 g carrots, chopped
60 g goat's cheese /cream
cheese
5 tbsp almond milk
40 g black olive pesto
2 tbsp olive oil
½ tsp ground black
pepper
A few fresh basil leaves
Rock salt, to taste

1. Cook the vegetables till they are soft and then process them to make a fine puree.
2. Add the rest of the ingredients and mix them in a blender to a smooth consistency.

Pumpkin Spread: Yellow Butter ✿

Serves: 4
Nutritional value:
1200 kcal (Carbs: 39 g,
Protein: 81 g, Fats: 80 g)

100 g steamed pumpkin
350 g goat's cheese
50 g pumpkin seeds
3 tbsp olive oil
Rock salt, to taste

1. Put all the ingredients into a blender and mix well till you get a fine cream.

Almond and Carrot Spread: Orange Butter ✣

Serves: 4
Nutritional value:
883 kcal (Carbs: 22 g,
Protein: 30 g, Fats: 75 g)

150 g almonds
100 g steamed carrots
1 tbsp walnut oil
1 pinch freshly grated
ginger
Rock salt, to taste
Freshly chopped coriander

1. Put the almonds, carrots, oil and ginger in a mixer and blend till it becomes creamy. Season with rock salt and fresh coriander.

Spelt Flatbread 🌱

Serves: 4
Nutritional value:
3690 kcal (Carbs: 800 g,
Protein: 100 g, Fats: 10 g)

1 kg fine spelt flour, plus
extra for kneading and
rolling
2 tbsp baking soda
2 tbsp sourdough powder
Rock salt, to taste
1 tsp coriander powder
1 tsp cumin powder
1 tsp aniseed powder

1. Mix all the ingredients with 500 ml of warm water and knead into dough. Leave for 30 minutes.

2. Separate into 70–75 g pieces and roll into round balls. Set aside for 15 minutes.

3. Flatten each ball with a rolling pin to a 1-cm-thick sheet. Leave them covered for about 20 minutes.

4. Preheat the oven to 180°C.

5. Fold the bread with a fork and bake for about 13–16 minutes. Serve the next day.

Soy Flatbread ✌

Serves: 4
Nutritional value:
2756 kcal (Carbs: 240 g,
Protein: 206 g, Fats: 108 g)

500 g soybean flour
250 g ground moong
flour
12 g salt
30 g cream of tartar
30 g egg substitute
(arrowroot)
800 ml warm water
1 tsp of finely ground
powder of coriander
fennel, anise and cumin
Olive oil for greasing

1. Preheat the oven to 190 °C.
2. Add all the ingredients in a large bowl and mix well.
3. Grease a baking tray with a small amount of olive oil. Sprinkle with a small amount of soybean flour.
4. Place the mixture in a pastry bag and form the dough into a spiral design. Bake for 13 minutes.
5. Let the bread rest for a day after baking before eating.

Conclusion

One of my earliest memories of food is sitting next to my grandmother while she ground all our masalas on the *silbatta* (grinding stone).

As I've mentioned before, my mother was a working woman. One day—I don't remember when exactly, I must have been five—she ended up with a slipped disc. Since my sister was quite young at that time, Mummy couldn't take care of both of us. So she sent me to live with my grandmother for a while. That resulted in all those afternoons sitting beside her as she ground and prepared her masalas for lunch or pickles for the rest of the year. She would entertain me with stories while she worked, and the hours would just melt away. Having eaten the food she made all those years ago with her home-ground masalas, I realize now how we've shortchanged ourselves with adulterated masalas without knowing what all has gone into them. Indian food tastes best when we use a concoction of good quality spices we've made at home. The sound of the mixer is not as satisfying or satiating as that of the grinding stone. However, I realize that doing that is not convenient any more. My cook at home will surely resign the day I ask him to make masalas of his own. I just make sure I buy the best quality masalas and spices; not compromising on the aromas and taste is key to enhance the flavours of anything you cook. But the joy my grandma took in cooking Mangalorean food is why it tasted so good.

Another person who's has a huge impact on my cooking skills is Charu Mehta. Growing up, my mother encouraged us to indulge in all kinds of extracurricular activities. And cooking was one of them. At the age of thirteen, I was enrolled in cooking classes conducted by Charu Aunty. My favourite part of the classes was the end because she would let us eat everything we cooked. She was an excellent teacher—patient, skilful and kind. She made me fall in love with cooking and gave me the confidence that I could be useful in—no, *rule* the kitchen.

With everything that my grandma, Mom and Charu Aunty taught me and what I've learnt on my own, I'm now quite adept at knowing the difference between good food and stuff that they tell us is good, but frankly isn't. That's why only a few have made it to my list of favourite restaurants. Those few seconds between biting into my food and ingesting it have been some of the happiest moments of my life. Every single one of these restaurants has made me feel that way with every dish I've ordered. The food they serve is complemented by their ambience, location and décor and add to a complete dining experience for my family and me: Black Cat in Lake Como, Italy, serves divine Italian food, and a view of the lake to match. The three Michelin star restaurant Alain Ducasse in Monaco is known for its French cuisine that goes beyond foie gras and lobster. Le Petite Maison in London offers French Mediterranean and Niçoise cuisine. And it has a branch in Dubai now, so that's brought good food closer to home. Their Quinoa and Lentil Salad as well as the Crab Salad are dishes I wish I could replicate. Dinner by Heston Blumenthal in London is an epicurean's delight. The Roast Halibut in Green Sauce just melts in the mouth. Innovative dishes like the Meat Fruit, and the Brown Bread Ice Cream (served with salted butter caramel, pear and malted yeast syrup) are worth the binge . . . Sunday or not! Speaking of which, my Sunday binges are not to show off, but to show people how much I love food, and that even I let go every week. To maintain a healthy weight and body, discipline is key, and one must have a 'cheat day' to get back to the 'regimen' without regret. Food must be relished for your soul to be nourished and satiated. I love visiting Wasabi and Nobu all over the world for their Japanese new-style sashimi, the Dover Sole in Ponzu Sauce and Rock Shrimp. In New York, Jaiya Thai makes the best Tom Kha, Green Curry and Mango Sticky Rice.

I hope you get a chance to eat these restaurants some day. Till then, enjoy making my healthy, yummy recipes and let me know what you thought of them on Instagram and Twitter. Better yet, upload your own video of making one of them and tag me in it. I'd love your feedback.

Acknowledgements

Milee Ashwarya, sorry for driving you up the wall, but I can't thank you enough for pushing me or this book would not have seen the light of day. Phew!

Parita, for helping me put pen to 'paper'—literally! And for all the late hours and calls. I couldn't have done this without you.

Anishi, my manager and best friend, you will always be a part of all the acknowledgements, because you bring the 'method' to my 'madness'. I'm proud to be a part of #Bethetribe.

Thank you, nutritionist Jaydeep Bhuta for your expertise in helping me with the nitty gritty of the nutritional values. Your contribution has been very valuable.

Last but not the least, my mom, mom-in-law, Pratibha Aunty and all the other fabulous cooks who have fed my soul. I remember every flavour and all the love to came with every dish still. Love you all so much!

A Note on the Author

SHILPA SHETTY KUNDRA is a renowned film and TV actor, businesswoman, author of *The Great Indian Diet*, entrepreneur and health enthusiast. She has always been a trendsetter, be it fashion or ideas. She is the first Indian actor to have her own successful YouTube channel and soon to be launched subscription-based app on fitness and overall wellness. A true influencer in the world of health and fitness, she plays this role very responsibly and passionately. She believes it is the right of every individual to enjoy good health in the right way.

YOU MAY ALSO LIKE

The Great Indian Diet
Busting the Big Fat Myth

Shilpa Shetty Kundra and Luke Coutinho

Why run after the West when we already have the best?

Join Shilpa Shetty and Luke Coutinho as they tell you just how nutritious your locally grown and sourced ingredients are and that there's no need to look beyond borders to tailor the perfect diet. The book touches upon various food categories and not only tells you how to take care of your nutritional intake but also how to burn fat in the process. The combined experience of a professional nutritionist and an uber-fit celebrity who lives by the diet will open your eyes to why Indian food is the best in the world.

Health/PB